SUCCEED IN

Public Administration

STUDENT BOOK

N6

Enock Mukwindidza

OXFORD
UNIVERSITY PRESS
SOUTH AFRICA

Oxford University Press is a department of the University of Oxford.
It furthers the University's objective of excellence in research, scholarship,
and education by publishing worldwide. Oxford is a registered trade mark of
Oxford University Press in the UK and in certain other countries.

Published in South Africa by
Oxford University Press Southern Africa (Pty) Limited

Vasco Boulevard, Goodwood, N1 City, Cape Town, South Africa, 7460
P O Box 12119, N1 City, Cape Town, South Africa, 7463

Oxford Succeed in Public Administration N6 Student Book

ISBN 978 01 907 20490

Second impression 2021

Publisher: Yolandi Farham
Editor: Sarah Middleton
Proofreader: Kathleen Sutton
Indexer: Sanet le Roux
Designer: Gisela Strydom
Cover designer: Cindy Armstrong
Typesetter: Aptara, Inc.
Printed and bound by Bidvest Data

The authors and publisher gratefully acknowledge permission to reproduce copyright material
in this book.

Every effort has been made to trace copyright holders, but if any copyright infringements have
been made, the publisher would be grateful for information that would enable any omissions or
errors to be corrected in subsequent impressions.

CONTENTS

MODULE 7

GOVERNMENTAL RELATIONSHIPS

HOW TO USE THIS BOOK

Welcome to the Oxford Succeed series for TVET Colleges. *Succeed in Public Administration N6* provides you with everything you need to excel. This page will help you to understand how the book works.

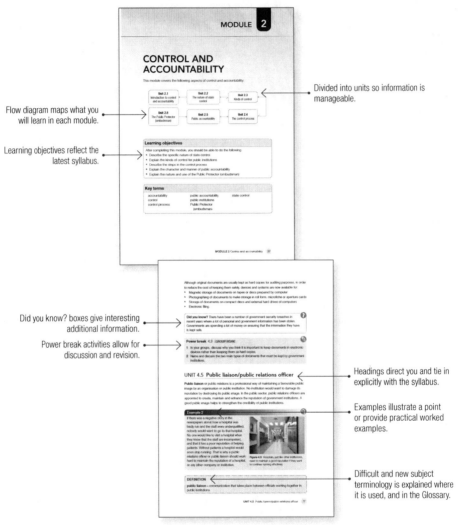

Divided into units so information is manageable.

Flow diagram maps what you will learn in each module.

Learning objectives reflect the latest syllabus.

Did you know? boxes give interesting additional information.

Power break activities allow for discussion and revision.

Headings direct you and tie in explicitly with the syllabus.

Examples illustrate a point or provide practical worked examples.

Difficult and new subject terminology is explained where it is used, and in the Glossary.

Other features:
- Relevant Case studies and articles bring information to life.
- Key points highlight core information, useful when studying.
- Diagrams, illustrations and photos provide information visually.
- At the end of every module, concise responses to the learning objectives are provided as a summary to use when studying.
- An Assessment section provides test and exam practice.

GENERIC, ADMINISTRATIVE AND MANAGEMENT FUNCTIONS

This module covers the following aspects of generic, administrative and management functions:

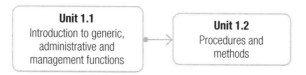

Unit 1.1
Introduction to generic, administrative and management functions

Unit 1.2
Procedures and methods

Learning objectives

After completing this module, you should be able to do the following:
- Provide a schematic presentation of generic, administrative and management functions
- Describe the development of work procedures
- Explain the necessity of formal procedures
- Explain the reasons for written procedures and methods
- Explain factors necessitating the revision of procedures
- Describe factors resisting change
- Explain who is responsible for developing and revising new procedures and methods
- Explain the techniques for analysis in the study of procedures and methods
- Explain the possible use of aids in revising procedures.

Key terms

administrative functions	management functions	resistance to change
formal procedures	methods	work procedures
generic	procedures	

Starting point

Some places of work are more dangerous than others, but every workplace must have health and safety regulations in place. Work safety procedures are generally written guidelines that define how tasks should be performed while minimising risks to people, equipment and the environment. The purpose of a work safety procedure is to reduce health and safety risks in the workplace and to reduce the likelihood of an injury.

Figure 1.1 To prevent or minimise workplace accidents, it is important that proper workplace safety procedures are put in place and followed.

Different types of workplace safety procedures and instructions exist in most workplaces. They include the following:
- Procedures relating to how chemicals must be handled and used
- Procedures relating to how objects are to be lifted and moved safely
- Procedures relating to fire, hot liquids and other dangerous materials
- Procedures relating to the installation, repair and maintenance of electrical equipment.

In this module, we briefly introduce generic, administrative and management functions. You will also learn about the different methods and procedures that are necessary for the effective functioning of public institutions.

UNIT 1.1 Introduction to generic, administrative and management functions

In Public Administration N5 you learned about **generic**, administrative and management functions. In this unit, we revisit these functions and provide, as introduction, a schematic presentation of all six generic, administrative and management functions that take place in government institutions. The **administrative functions** are necessary to achieve the objectives of government through its various departments and institutions.

How many of the generic, administrative and **management functions** do you remember? Discuss them in your groups.

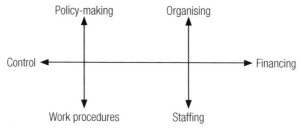

Figure 1.2 Schematic representation of generic, administrative and management functions.

Power break 1.1 GROUP WORK

Visit your local police station and comment on at least one of the administrative functions in place there. Explain how they are implemented. For example, do they have a computerised system for keeping records or do they use paper (hard copies)?

UNIT 1.2 Procedures and methods

Key aspects of procedures and methods to be discussed in this unit include the development of work procedures, the necessity for formal procedures and the reasons why it is important to have written procedures and methods. You will also learn about the various factors affecting the revision of procedures, the reasons for resisting change and the people who are responsible for revising and developing new **procedures** and **methods**. Furthermore, you will learn about the aids that are necessary for revising procedures.

> **DEFINITIONS**
>
> **generic** – not specific, relating to a general class or group
>
> **administrative functions** – the process of organising people and resources in order to improve efficiency and effectiveness
>
> **management functions** – the duties of people running an organisation
>
> **procedures** – systems of established steps that are taken to achieve an objective or to accomplish a task
>
> **methods** – processes that are used to achieve an objective

To function efficiently and effectively, government institutions need to have proper procedures and methods to guide employees when carrying out their daily activities. Without proper procedures and methods, the provision of services by government might be affected because employees could do as they wish rather than doing their jobs.

Clear procedures and methods help to ensure co-operation among employees and for the organisation to successfully achieve its objectives. It is important to have specific procedures for each task in order to avoid wasting time and resources. Procedures and methods should be constantly updated to keep them relevant.

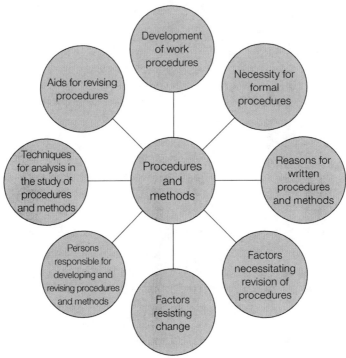

Figure 1.3 The aspects of procedures and methods that will be covered in this module.

1.2.1 Development of work procedures

In any institution, there are different procedures that are followed when dealing with different situations. These could be procedures to complete a task, to launch a grievance or to embark on a strike action. You might wonder why some strike actions are considered "illegal". This is because they are carried out without following proper procedures. **Work procedures** are comprised of certain steps that must be followed to achieve certain objectives. Think of the steps that you must go through to obtain a driver's licence, or to become a doctor or a pilot.

DEFINITION

work procedures – the process through which a task is carried out

Work procedures involve a fixed step-by-step sequence of activities that must be followed when performing a given task. Depending on the nature of the work, some procedures are more detailed than others. It is important to have detailed work procedures because they are less likely to have room for mistakes and deviations.

In South Africa, organisations and institutions are required by law to develop appropriate work procedures that will guide them when dealing with different situations in the workplace. Work procedures set out the steps to be followed when carrying out tasks in the workplace. Before work procedures are developed, those who may be affected (employees) should be consulted. Some of the situations that require proper procedures to be followed in the workplace are provided in the Labour Relations Act, No. 66 of 1995, and they include:

- Collective bargaining
- Unfair dismissal
- Conflict resolution
- Strikes and lockouts
- Grievance handling
- Retrenchment
- Disciplinary issues
- Training and development
- Health and safety.

Figure 1.4 Protective clothing is an aspect of health and safety.

When procedures are developed they must be followed. Apart from the procedures that are followed by an employee when completing a task, procedures are also developed when:

- A company or institution is established for the first time
- An institution or organisation is expanding
- New technology is being introduced
- Existing procedures are being reviewed
- There is a shift in the way the organisation is operating or in policy.

When developing work procedures, it is important that both the employer and the employee are involved. When both the employer and the employee are involved in developing procedures conflict is minimised and they both understand what they are expected to do.

In government departments, appropriate work procedures can be developed by "work study officials". These are officials who are appointed to develop appropriate work procedures for different government departments and institutions. Civil servants, or government employees, are required to follow proper procedures when carrying out their tasks.

Government has the task of developing appropriate work procedures to carry out legislative, executive and administrative functions. Work procedures help public institutions to be effective, efficient and to be consistent when carrying out their tasks.

When developing work procedures, the following must be considered:

- The nature of the task to be performed
- The provision of existing policy
- The complexity of the task
- The type and size of the organisation
- The safety of the employees.

Figure 1.5 Many elements need to be considered when developing procedures.

Two types of procedures exist in the public sector:

1. Procedures that must be followed when government decides on a major policy shift. For example, the change from Further Education and Training colleges (FET) to Technical, Vocational Education and Training colleges (TVET).
2. Procedures that must be followed when doing day-to-day tasks. For example, TVET colleges need to follow specific procedures for them to be effective and efficient at the level of day-to-day functioning.

At the workplace, it is the duty of management to provide proper training to the employees and officials on the procedures that are required when performing their tasks. Employees should know what disciplinary procedures will be taken if they are found guilty of misconduct or deviation.

Key points:

- Procedures give guidance to how a task ought to be performed. They help to promote efficiency, effectiveness and productivity.
- Procedures must be relevant and written in detail.

Case study

From FET to TVET colleges

The renaming of FET (Further Education and Training) colleges to TVET (Technical Vocational Education and Training) colleges was a result of the announcement by the Minister of Higher Education and Training, Dr Blade Nzimande, at the launch of the departmental "White Paper on Post-School Education and Training" on 15 January 2014. The re-naming process had started early in 2012 with the passing of the Further Education and Training Colleges Amendment Bill (B24, 2012). The bill included a ratifying clause that redefined the term "college" as used in the South African education system. From this bill, a "college" in the South African context would mean:

Figure 1.6 FET colleges were renamed to become TVET colleges.

1 A public college that is established or declared as:
  - A technical and vocational education and training college; or
  - A community education and training college

2 A private college that is established and declared or registered under this Act

Following the announcement by Dr Blade Nzimande, all private and public FET colleges would now be re-defined as TVET colleges. The Department of Higher Education and Training (DHET) and all FET colleges in the country had to start with the processes and procedures required to systematically re-name themselves to reflect the official change which had been implemented by the DHET.

Questions

1 Based on what you learned in N4 (Module 6) explain what you understand by a "White Paper".
2 Why do you think a "White Paper" was necessary in re-naming FET colleges? Why do you think this was the right procedure?
3 When did the re-naming of FET colleges begin?
4 Explain the meaning of a "college" in the South African education system.
5 Discuss the procedures and processes that you think were taken in changing from FET to TVET colleges. You can consult your campus management in this regard.

Power break 1.2 GROUP WORK

Discuss the procedures that new students who intend to register at your college should follow. In your discussion highlight the advantages and disadvantages of the procedures. How can the registration procedures at your college be improved?

1.2.2 Necessity for formal procedures

The necessity for **formal procedures** is usually associated with the American mechanical engineer, F.W. Taylor (1856–1915). Taylor observed workers loading cast-iron bars onto a train and realised that their productivity was low. He wanted to know how the situation could be improved. He then stipulated four changes that could increase productivity in the work environment as follows:

- Only workers who qualify to do the work must be appointed
- Work procedures must be set out in detail
- Top wages must be paid to workers
- Workers must have sufficient rest periods so that they do not suffer from lack of energy.

Figure 1.7 Proper work procedures ensure that work gets done efficiently.

Taylor's stipulations showed that when work procedures are streamlined they can result in the following advantages:

- Improved flow of work
- Better utilisation of labour
- Reduction in the costs of goods and services
- Increased productivity.

Taylor's observation shows that lack of procedures can lead to underutilisation of employees, reduced productivity and poor service delivery. It is also costly to the organisation and it can cause chaos when individual employees do as they please.

Below are some more reasons for having formal procedures:

- They provide guidance for day-to-day operations of an organisation
- They address the issue of accountability, which is an important aspect in the public sector
- They help managers to control events in advance and prevent the organisation and employees from making costly mistakes
- They help to connect the vision and goals of the organisation to its internal operations
- Employees are made aware of the risks that are associated with their tasks and how they can avoid injury while performing their tasks
- They provide a means of communicating information to new employees
- They set rules and guidelines for decision-making in routine situations so that employees and managers do not need to continually ask senior managers what to do
- They allow employees to be treated fairly and equally
- They allow management to have accepted methods of dealing with complaints and misunderstandings and to avoid favouritism.

> **DEFINITION**
>
> **formal procedures** – steps that are well established or written and are used to achieve or accomplish a task

1.2.3 Reasons for written procedures and methods

Procedures are an essential element of any organisation. It is not always easy for employees to remember how they ought to carry out their day-to-day activities. Written procedures provide a source of reference when employees do not remember how to carry out certain tasks or what steps to follow when completing a task. It is important that employees read the necessary procedures for themselves and understand them. Procedures and methods can be explained in detail in printed manuals and codes.

Written procedures and methods have the following advantages:

- They provide a source of reference when employees do not know how to carry out tasks. For example, employees can refer to a manual or a code where the procedures are written.
- Employees do not need to constantly ask management how to carry out given tasks, they just refer to a manual or a code
- They help to avoid chaos when employees use different procedures to carry out tasks at the same institution
- They help to ensure efficiency and effectiveness and to reduce wastage of resources
- They help to improve quality control because variations are minimised
- They help to ensure that a common goal is achieved
- They help to ensure consistency. For example, employees who commit a similar act of misconduct are likely to be treated the same if the disciplinary procedures are written down. If one employee is fired for stealing but another employee is only suspended for the same misconduct, it would not be fair.
- They help to ensure the safety of employees. For example, employees will know how to carry out tasks that can put their health and safety at risk, such as the correct way of working with heavy machinery.
- All new employees are trained in the same way
- They help to ensure uniformity, especially where procedures are the same for different divisions in an organisation. For example, there should be similar enrolment procedures at a college with six campuses. This is so that staff and students understand what they need to do and no information goes missing.
- They help to provide clarity on how tasks need to be carried out. This is necessary especially for new employees.
- They can be used for training new employees or when a new technology is introduced
- They should be drafted (written down) as soon as possible. It is easier to review written procedures and methods than unwritten ones.
- They can easily be referred to when management exercises control over its employees.

Figure 1.8 Policies and procedures are usually written in manuals, which should be available to employees.

Example of a formal disciplinary procedure

Formal disciplinary procedures consist of a series of fixed steps that need to be followed. The following is an example of steps that are taken during a formal disciplinary procedure.

Step 1:
Verbal warning

Step 2:
First written warning

Step 3:
Second written warning

Step 4:
Final written warning

Step 5:
Dismissal or action short of dismissal

Power break 1.3 **PAIR WORK**

1 Why do you think it is important to have written procedures?
2 Visit a local public institution, a college, hospital or a police station and find out what the institution considers a gross misconduct. Write down the disciplinary procedure of the institution you have visited.

1.2.4 Factors necessitating revision of procedures

The world today is going through a lot of changes both socially, economically and technologically. This is caused by many factors. In countries such as South Africa the demand for better services such as health, education, public transport and good infrastructure continue to increase faster than the ability of government to provide them. To remain relevant, procedures should be constantly revised. There are many factors that necessitate the revision of procedures, as discussed below.

In this section we will be looking at the following factors that necessitate a revision of procedures:

- The needs and expectations of the people
- Technological development
- Increase in population
- Outdated methods and procedures
- Scientific progress
- Changes in legislation
- Development of the administrative and management sciences.

The needs and expectations of the people

After the 1994 democratic elections in South Africa, the needs and expectations of many citizens changed drastically. To some, democracy meant a change of life for the better. Today, more than twenty years after the democratic elections, most South Africans still want their needs to be addressed. They expect the government to address the issues relating to:

- The housing crisis in urban areas
- HIV/AIDS and health issues
- Unemployment
- Working conditions
- Access to service delivery
- Transparency and accountability
- Corruption
- Poverty
- Racism and sexism
- Violence and crime.

Figure 1.9 Poverty is an issue that people expect the government to address.

When addressing the needs of the people, the following must be considered:

- Changes in the attitude of the public
- Changes in demography/population
- Changes in the views of the current government.

Technological development

The development of technology has drastically changed our way of life. Think of how the cell phone has transformed the communication system in our society. By using smart phones people can send photos and messages instantly or download music. The development of technology has changed the way areas such as hospitals, schools and farms operate. It has also changed the way we travel.

Figure 1.10 Technological developments mean that modes of transport, such as trains, are much faster and cleaner than they were in the past.

Increase in population

An increase in population means a higher demand for goods and services. Government must find ways of providing for the ever-increasing demand for goods and services.

Example 1

In 1996, the population of Gauteng was just under 8 million people. In 2001, it was over 9 million. By 2011, the population had jumped up to over 12 million people. That increase has meant that infrastructure and government services have needed to expand to provide for the people living in that province. Think about how many people use roads, water and refuse removal services. With millions more people living in an area, roads will need maintenance more often, there needs to be more water provided and more refuse removal than ever before.

See the table below for the population increase in South Africa, per province, for three census years.

Table 1.1 Population increase in South Africa

PROVINCE	CENSUS 1996	CENSUS 2001	CENSUS 2011
Western Cape	3 956 875	4 524 335	5 822 734
Eastern Cape	6 147 244	6 278 651	6 562 053
Northern Cape	1 011 864	991 919	1 145 861
Free State	2 633 504	2 706 775	2 745 590
KwaZulu-Natal	8 572 302	9 584 129	10 267 300
North West	2 727 223	2 984 098	3 509 953
Gauteng	7 834 125	9 388 854	12 272 263
Mpumalanga	3 123 869	3 365 554	4 039 939
Limpopo	4 576 566	4 995 462	5 404 868
South Africa	**40 583 573**	**44 819 778**	**51 770 560**

Source: Statistics South Africa. https://www.statssa.gov.za/publications/P03014/P030142011.pdf (Access date: 15 August 2017).

Outdated methods and procedures

In the previous section you learned that procedures must be relevant. Outdated methods and procedures should be revised to keep them relevant. Using outdated methods and procedures is like using medication that is expired. It can be harmful. When methods and procedures are outdated, it is difficult to achieve objectives, and they need to be revised and updated.

Scientific progress

There has been significant progress in science and technology in the 21st century. This has resulted in the demand for highly qualified personnel in both the public and private sectors. In response to the demand for highly qualified personnel in various fields such as education, health, security and engineering, many students are enrolling at universities and TVET colleges to get relevant qualifications. Enrolment procedures at these universities and TVET colleges must be revised so as to remain relevant in the wake of increased demand.

Changes in legislation

Policies and procedures complement each other. A change in policy must be followed by a revision of procedures. This is necessary to keep procedures relevant. For example, the proposed funding model for university education in South Africa requires many procedures at universities to be revised.

Development of the administrative and management sciences

Research in public administration has shown that administrative and managerial functions in public institutions require specific skills that cannot be learned through experience only. Theoretical knowledge is also vital for skills development.

Example 2

Revising procedures in public institutions requires particular skills that are acquired through education. It is necessary to be able to think analytically and to do sound research. It is for this reason that public institutions are interested in employing supervisors who are well educated and trained.

1.2.5 Factors resisting change

Most people do not like change. The saying, "Better the devil you know than the devil you don't know" shows how people are prepared to resist change. Although the world today is experiencing a lot of changes because of socio-economic and political factors, people are afraid of change. Even politicians do not usually want to embrace change.

Sometimes change is a result of development of new technology, research and innovation or increase in population. It is usually difficult for organisations to avoid change because new ideas promote growth. Whatever the reason for change, people still resist it. Why do people resist change?

"What if we don't change at all ...
and something magical just happens?"

Figure 1.11 Resistance to change can slow things down and decrease efficiency.

Factors that are usually associated with **resistance to change** are briefly discussed below:

Loss of status or job security:

Change many result in some people losing their jobs and status especially when an organisation is rebranding. Employees will always resist change if their status and job security are not guaranteed.

Fear of the unknown:

People do not usually know what the future holds for them. In order to be certain, they would rather resist any changes that may take place.

Peer pressure:

Some people resist change because their workmates do not like the change. Such people do not know why they are resisting the change.

Climate of mistrust:

Trust plays a big role in the success of a business. If employees do not trust the motive for the change or the key decision-makers, they are likely to resist the change.

Fear of failure:

When changes require mastering new skills, for example, as a result of new technology, resistance is likely to take place because people feel that they will not know how to use new technology and they will fail.

Poor communication and engagement:

Changes within an organisation or institution start with decision-makers. If the reasons for the changes are not well communicated and explained and if the employees are not involved from the start, they will resist the change.

> **DEFINITION**
>
> **resistance to change –** the act of refusing or opposing transformation

Poor timing:

Change brings a lot uncertainty. It is important that the timing does not disadvantage other members within the organisation.

Exclusion:

If employees feel that they have been excluded from giving their input regarding certain changes within the organisation, they may feel offended and will resist the change.

Figure 1.12 Communication is essential in any company or institution. If new ideas are not communicated to employees properly they may resist change and cause delays.

Self-interest:

Some people do not want change because the status quo benefits them. They want to maintain the status quo to advance their personal interests. Such people will resist change that may not be in their own interests.

Institutional politics:

Politicians and officials who have the power to change policy may refuse to amend or repeal policies because they fear that new policies may not be good for them. In this case, employees will remain powerless because they do not have capacity to amend or repeal policies themselves.

Implementation:

Although the suggestion for change might look good on paper, it may not be practically possible to implement it.

Prohibitive costs:

The cost of machinery and the process to effect the change can be costly to implement.

1.2.6 Persons responsible for developing and revising procedures and methods

By now you should know why it is important for both the employer and employees to be involved in developing and revising procedures: it helps to minimise conflict. People who are responsible for developing and revising procedures and methods include the following:

- **Supervisors and managers:** They evaluate procedures to see if they can be implemented in the organisation.
- **Managing directors and executive members:** They encourage staff to look out for better procedures.
- **Employees or officials:** They should be involved in developing and revising new procedures and methods.
- **Personnel officers:** They look out for shortcomings, locate the problems and find ways to fix them.
- **Clients:** They provide suggestions for improvement to the organisation. Suggestions from clients should not be ignored.

Figure 1.13 Clients' suggestions should be listened to and not ignored.

1.2.7 Techniques for analysis in the study of procedures and methods

Various approaches and techniques can be used to analyse and improve procedures and methods in an organisation. In this section, we discuss the analytical approach and the necessary techniques:

- Graphic techniques
- Visual techniques
- Mathematical techniques
- Linear techniques
- Exact techniques
- Simulation techniques.

Analytical approach

The analytical approach is defined as "the use of an appropriate process to break down a problem into elements that are necessary to solve it". The approach consists of a sequence of questions that are arranged logically and that provide necessary information on various areas that need to be addressed. The analytical approach can be applied to all work situations.

There are specific analytical techniques that can be used to assist in improving procedures and methods in an organisation. The analytical techniques are briefly discussed below.

Figure 1.14 The analytical approach uses analysis to approach issues that need to be solved.

Graphic techniques

Graphic techniques use symbols, in a diagrammatic form, to show the steps that are followed in a procedure. Graphic symbols represent the actual flow of work in an organisation. They can be used to find any shortfalls in work procedures that need to be revised. Graphic techniques help employees and officials understand work procedures better. Graphic techniques can be referred to as flowcharts.

Examples of flowcharts or graphic techniques include the following:

- Basic flowcharts are the simplest form of flowcharts.
- Process charts represent sequence of events, activities or tasks up to completion of the entire procedure.
- Work process charts record major events in a sequence of processes for different activities in an organisation.
- Flow process charts graphically show the flow of a product and what happens at each handling point until it reaches the factory.
- Flow diagrams provide an indication of the flow of an object through an organisation or institution.
- String, wire and scale models indicate the real position of objects such as the position of a machine or a building.
- Man-machine process charts show workload and usage ratios between employees and machines to determine which machines or man hours are not fully utilised.

• Simultaneous motion cycle charts (SIMO charts) are used when extremely fast hand reactions are required to determine the workload of an employee.

Figure 1.15 Flowcharts show the steps that should be followed in any procedure.

Visual techniques

Visual techniques can be used when a real situation needs to be duplicated. Often a picture or a model is easier to understand than an explanation of what something will look like. For example, scale models are small versions of real constructions, which are made to look realistic so that people can visualise how a building will look.

Figure 1.16 A scale model can be used to present what a building may look like when it is built.

Mathematical techniques

This technique is used when an output needs to be determined by mathematical calculations.

For example, if you wanted to know whether there was an increase in the percentage of female students enrolling in TVET colleges in a particular province you would use a mathematical calculation. By looking at the numbers of female enrolments at TVET colleges in a certain year you could determine the percentage of female students and compare that percentage to previous years. If the percentage is higher in more recent years, then the percentage is increasing.

Linear techniques

These are directed at representing future possibilities during the planning of activities. They consist of a combination of mathematical and visual techniques. For example, the plan of a house shows the use of linear techniques.

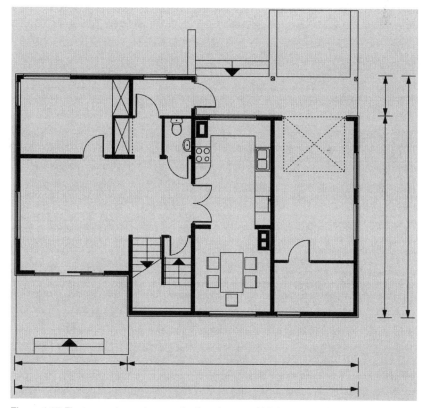

Figure 1.17 The image above shows a plan for a house, which is an example of a linear technique.

Exact techniques

These are techniques that are used to measure the exact work done and the exact time taken to do the work. They can be used to determine the performance of an average employee or worker. Sometimes employers will ask their employees to keep a record of their exact tasks and the time it took to do them. This is called a work log. When the employer reviews the employee's work log they can see how efficient and fast their employee is, and they can also see the diversity of tasks that the employee performs.

Simulation techniques

Simulation techniques imitate the operation of a real-world system over a period of time. You will probably have heard of a flight simulator, where new pilots learn to fly a plane without the danger of actually being in an aircraft.

1.2.8 Aids for revising procedures

Before we discuss aids for revising procedures it is important that we revisit the observations made by Taylor. You have learned that after his observations, Taylor stipulated four changes that could increase productivity. Do you remember the four stipulations that Taylor made? What advantages did Taylor's four stipulations have? After Taylor's observations, the following developments emerged:
- The stipulations were later adopted by both the private and public sectors
- Functionaries were appointed to examine organisational systems and work procedures
- South Africa now appoints functionaries who are known as "work study officers", "efficiency officers" and "management advisory officers" at all the three levels of government.

The main reasons for appointing work study officers are based on the observations made by Taylor. They help to:
- Eliminate wastage of time in man hours
- Increase productivity
- Make the flow of work quicker and more efficient.

Functionaries who are appointed as work study officers can be private consultants or they can be trained by the institution or organisation. Public institutions prefer to train their own functionaries rather than to hire private consultants. There are some advantages and disadvantages for hiring private consultants. The following are some of them:

Advantages
- Private consultants are more advanced in specific fields and this helps them to develop and apply specific techniques that can improve work procedures
- Private consultants can use specialists who are skilled in specific fields to revise procedures.

Disadvantages

- Private consultants are not familiar with the extent of the services provided by public institutions
- Private consultants have little knowledge of the political dynamics in the public sector
- They are not familiar with the control functions used in the public sector
- Techniques and practices of private consultants differ considerably from those of the public sector
- Private consultants demand high remunerations, which the public institutions cannot afford.

Personal qualities of the functionary

Public institutions would prefer to train their own functionaries. When choosing their own functionaries, public institutions need to ensure that the candidate they train is able to perform well in the position of functionary.

He or she must be:

- A good communicator
- A people person
- Able to understand issues quickly
- Able to think analytically.

Key point: Public institutions prefer to train their own functionaries than to hire private consultants.

Power break 1.4 GROUP WORK

1 Revise the various techniques you have learned in this section and give practical examples of each one of them.
2 Draw a process chart showing the registration process at your college.
3 Give real-life examples where mathematical techniques are used.
4 What do you think is the main purpose of the various techniques you have studied in this section?

WHAT DO WE KNOW AND WHERE TO NEXT...

Revisiting the learning objectives

Now that you have worked your way through this module, let's see if you have achieved the learning objectives that we set out at the beginning. In the table that follows we summarise the main concepts that you should know for each learning objective.

Learning objectives	What you have learned
Provide a schematic presentation of generic, administrative and management functions	See the schematic presentation in Unit 1.1
Describe the development of work procedures	Two types of procedures exist: • Procedures that must be followed when government decides on a major policy shift • Procedures that must be followed when doing day-to-day tasks. When developing work procedures, the following must be considered: • The nature of the task to be performed • The provision of existing policy • The complexity of the task • Type and size of the organisation • Safety of the employees.
Explain the necessity of formal procedures	The necessity for formal procedures as streamlined by Taylor is that they can result in: • Improved flow of work • Better utilisation of labour • Reduction in the costs of goods and services • Increased productivity. Other reasons why formal procedures are necessary include the following: • They provide guidance for day-to-day operations of an organisation. • They address the issue of accountability, which is an important aspect in the public sector. • They help managers to control events in advance and prevent the organisation and employees from making costly mistakes.

Learning objectives	What you have learned
	• They help to connect the vision and goals of the organisation to its internal operations. • Employees are made aware of the risks that are associated with their tasks and how they can avoid injury while performing their tasks. • They provide a means of communicating information to new employees. • They set rules and guidelines for decision-making in routine situations so that employees and managers do not need to continually ask senior managers what to do. • They allow employees to be treated fairly and equally. • They allow management to have accepted methods of dealing with complaints and misunderstandings and to avoid favouritism.
Explain the reasons for written procedures and methods	Reasons for written procedures include the following: • They provide a source of reference when employees do not know how to carry out tasks. For example, employees will always refer to a manual or a code where the procedures are written. • Employees do not need to constantly ask management how to carry our given tasks, they just refer to a manual or a code. • They help to avoid chaos when employees use different procedures to carry out tasks at the same institution. • They help to ensure efficiency and effectiveness and to reduce wastage of resources. • They help to improve quality control because variations are minimised. • They help to ensure that a common goal is achieved. • They help to ensure consistency. For example, employees who commit a similar act of misconduct are likely to be treated the same if the disciplinary procedures are written down. • They help to ensure the safety of employees. For example, employees will know how to carry out tasks that can put their health and safety at risk. • All new employees are trained in the same way. • They help to ensure uniformity especially where procedures are the same for different divisions in an organisation. For example, similar enrolment procedures are in place at a college with six campuses. • They help to provide clarity on how tasks need to be carried out. This is necessary especially for new employees. • They can be used for training new employees or when a new technology is introduced. • It is easier to review written procedures and methods than unwritten ones. • They can easily be referred to when management exercises control over its employees.
Explain factors necessitating the revision of procedures	Factors necessitating revision of procedures include the following: • The needs and expectations of the people • Technological development • Increase in population • Outdated methods and procedures • Scientific progress • Changes in legislation • Development of the administrative and management sciences.

Learning objectives	What you have learned
Describe factors resisting change	Factors that make people resist change include the following: • Loss of status or job security • Fear of the unknown • Peer pressure • Climate of mistrust • Fear of failure • Poor communication and lack of engagement • Poor timing • Exclusion • Self-interest • Institutional politics • Implementation • Prohibitive costs.
Explain who is responsible for developing and revising procedures and methods	The following people are responsible for developing and revising procedures: • Supervisors and managers • Managing directors and executive members • Employees or officials • Personnel officers • Clients.
Explain the techniques for analysis in the study of procedures and methods	Techniques for analysis in the study of procedures and methods include the following: • Graphic techniques • Visual techniques • Mathematical techniques • Linear techniques • Exact techniques • Simulation techniques.
Explain the possible use of aids in revising procedures	The possibility of using aids in revising procedures came as a result of the observations and stipulations by Taylor. • The stipulations were later adopted by both the private and public sectors. • Functionaries were appointed to examine organisational systems and work procedures. • South Africa now appoints functionaries who are known as "work study officers", "efficiency officers" and "management advisory officers" at all the three levels of government.

Assessment

True or false questions

Indicate whether the following statements are TRUE or FALSE. Choose the answer and write only "true" or "false" next to the question number.

1. People resist change because they are afraid of failure.
2. Only the management of an organisation is responsible for developing work procedures.
3. Streamlined work procedures can lead to a reduction in the cost of goods and services.
4. Procedures should be developed and constantly updated to keep them irrelevant.
5. The main reason for appointing work study officers is to eliminate waste in man hours and increase productivity.
6. The change from FET to TVET did not necessarily require strict procedures.
7. Taylor observed that the use of procedures led to overutilisation of workers.
8. Work procedure is not one of the main generic, administrative and management functions.
9. Work procedures involve a fixed step-by-step sequence of activities that must be followed when performing a given task.
10. Written procedures are not necessary if employees know what to do.

(10 × 2) [20]

Definitions

Define the following terms:

1. Analytical approach
2. Method
3. Exact technique
4. Formal procedure
5. Procedure

(5 × 2) [10]

Acronyms

What do the following acronyms mean?

1. DHET
2. SOP
3. FET
4. HIV/AIDS
5. TVET

(5 × 2) [10]

Match the columns

Match the term in Column A to the correct description in Column B.

Column A	Column B
1. Mathematical techniques	A. Trained functionary who examines the system of the organisation and gives suggestions for improvement
2. F.W. Taylor	B. Used when an output is to be determined by mathematical calculations
3. Work study officer	C. Represents a sequence of events, activities or tasks
4. Process charts	D. Look out for shortcomings, locate the problems and find ways to fix them
5. Personnel officers	E. Provides indication of the flow of an object through an organisation
	F. Developer of streamlined work procedure

(5 × 2) [10]

Short questions

Answer the following questions:

1. Name the techniques for analysis in the study of procedures and methods. (6 × 2) [12]
2. Name the persons who are responsible for developing and revising new procedures and methods. (5 × 2) [10]
3. Give four reasons why it is important to streamline work procedures. (4 × 2) [8]

Discussion questions

Answer the following questions:

1. Explain the factors that make people resist change. (20)
2. F.W. Taylor suggested four changes that should take place to improve production. Explain these changes. (8)
3. Certain factors necessitate the need to revise procedures. Discuss the factors that influence the revision of procedures. (20)
4. Explain why written procedures are necessary. (12)
5. Discuss five things that should be considered when developing work procedures. (10)

Grand total: 150

MODULE **2**

CONTROL AND ACCOUNTABILITY

This module covers the following aspects of control and accountability:

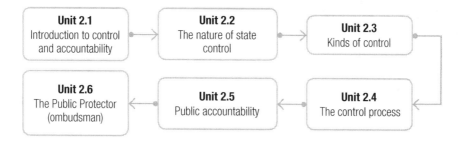

| Unit 2.1 Introduction to control and accountability | Unit 2.2 The nature of state control | Unit 2.3 Kinds of control |
| Unit 2.6 The Public Protector (ombudsman) | Unit 2.5 Public accountability | Unit 2.4 The control process |

Learning objectives

After completing this module, you should be able to do the following:
- Describe the specific nature of state control
- Explain the kinds of control for public institutions
- Describe the steps in the control process
- Explain the character and manner of public accountability
- Explain the nature and use of the Public Protector (ombudsman)

Key terms

accountability
control
control process

public accountability
public institutions
Public Protector
(ombudsman)

state control

Figure 2.1 Emma helps Musi to understand control and accountability.

Emma and Musi are studying Public Management at a TVET College in Cape Town. When they were revising for their mock examinations Musi wanted to know more about control and accountability, so he asked for Emma's help.

Emma explained to Musi that the functions of government officials must be controlled so that the officials do not abuse their authority. They must also be held accountable for their decisions, actions and policies. The reason that we have control and accountability is to make sure that government officials provide the necessary services to the public.

Emma also explained that the office of the Auditor-General is basically responsible for controlling the activities of government. Auditing is one way of controlling the activities of government. The office of the Auditor-General carries out different kinds of audits in all government departments and institutions to ensure efficiency and effectiveness.

In this module, you will learn more about control and accountability.

UNIT 2.1 Introduction to control and accountability

The main purpose of **control** and **accountability** in public administration is to ensure efficient and effective utilisation of resources and to enhance public service provision, good governance and development.

In previous levels you learned about the three arms of government; the legislature, the judiciary and the executive. It is not possible for members of the public to exercise legislative, judicial and executive functions. Government officials (functionaries) are either elected or appointed to perform these functions on behalf of the public and they must be accountable for their actions and decisions.

In South Africa, the concepts of control and accountability are supported by the Constitution. The list below shows some examples of where the Constitution supports control and accountability.

- Section 102 provides that Parliament must exercise control over the executive
- Section 165 declares that the judiciary is bound by the Constitution (this means the judiciary is accountable to the Constitution)
- Section 195 (f) provides that Public administration must be accountable. This means government must be accountable to the people (voters).

Sometimes public officials neglect their duties. The objective of control in the public sector is to ensure that public officials are held accountable for their actions. Control in the public sector consists of two parts:

- Internal control: takes place within government departments and institutions
- Giving account: involves giving an explanation as to why certain activities were done or not done. The explanation is given by a government official to the public and in public.

Example 1

Parliament must exercise control over the executive, as stated in Section 102 of the Constitution. What this means is that if the majority of the members of the National Assembly support a vote of no confidence in the President, she or he must resign. If the no confidence vote is directed against the Cabinet, the President must reconstitute the Cabinet.

DEFINITIONS

control – the process of ensuring that actual activities, actions or behaviour conform to set standards and procedures

accountability – taking full responsibility, by a person or organisation, for actions or decisions taken or not taken by providing an explanation and accepting responsibility for the action or decision

Services are often provided to communities through government institutions and departments. All citizens want their governments to provide them with quality services, so it is important that these institutions and departments are managed by competent people and that effective control mechanisms are put in place. Public officials must be held accountable for their actions, decisions and policies.

How is control and accountability implemented?

The office of the Auditor-General (AG) controls the activities of government institutions and departments through auditing. In February 2017, the AG's office released its audit report, which shows that fewer South African municipalities received clean audits than in 2016. The main reason for poor performance by most municipalities is a lack of control in key financial areas.

The report also shows that those in financial and supply chain management posts were not accepting accountability for their actions. This means that public officials working in municipalities do not understand the key policies, processes and procedures that are associated with the running of municipalities.

Figure 2.2 Auditing ensures that government departments and institutions are held financially accountable.

Did you know?

- A vote of no confidence on a state president or members of the executive is a system of control of Parliament over the executive.
- A budget speech is a way of giving account regarding public finance by the executive through the Minister of Finance.

Power break 2.1 GROUP WORK

In your groups, discuss control and accountability in respect of the following:

- The three arms of government
- The constitution
- The voters.

UNIT 2.2 **The nature of state control**

State control refers to the systems that are put in place by government to ensure uniformity, effectiveness and efficiency in the delivery of services. This means the government controls the operations of public institutions such as hospitals, schools and state enterprises. Government also exercises control over the functions of public institutions and government departments in order to minimise unethical behaviour by public officials. State control can also be referred to as governmental control.

It is important for organisations and institutions to have effective control systems to detect and regulate undesirable activities such as theft, corruption, delay in work and unco-operative attitudes.

Advantages of effective control are as follows:
- Mistakes can easily be identified and checked
- New challenges can be identified and addressed
- Deviations from set standards can immediately be identified and corrective measures can be taken promptly
- Actual work performance is easily compared with set standards against which accuracy is measured
- Resources are used more efficiently because wastage is constantly checked
- Employees are motivated when they know that their work will be evaluated and reported upon
- Order and discipline is ensured; undesirable activities such as theft, corruption and delays are checked in time
- Co-ordination of activities within the organisation is ensured.

In the public sector, there are several reasons why it is necessary to exercise control. The following are some of the reasons why it is important to exercise control over executive institutions.
- Public institutions are established by government to meet the needs, demands and requirements of the public. In this way, government maintains its control over policy, financing, organising, procedures and management of public purposes.
- The use of public funds must be controlled. Funds made available by Parliament are public funds that are kept in trust until they are spent for specific purposes that benefit the public.
- It is essential to minimise unethical behaviour such as theft, bribery, corruption, nepotism and wastage. Such unethical behaviour leads to lack of growth, chaos and poor service delivery. The public may respond by engaging in service delivery protests.
- Control must be exercised over the actions and decisions of public officials to ensure legitimacy and legality.

> **DEFINITION**
>
> **state control** – systems that are put in place by government to ensure uniformity, efficiency and effectiveness in the delivery of services

- The objectives of government include maintenance of law and order, welfare and peace. Control helps to ensure that the objectives of government are maintained.
- By improving the systems of control and accountability, integrity in the public sector is maintained.

Power break 2.2 CLASS WORK

Why do you think it is necessary to have control systems in TVET Colleges in South Africa? Debate this question in class and give reasons to support your views.

UNIT 2.3 **Kinds of control**

Control and accountability complement each other. Control helps to ensure that those in public offices are held accountable for their actions and decisions. The Auditor-General is responsible for controlling the use of public funds at all government levels in South Africa through the process of auditing.

Although the control process in government takes place in different forms, there are basically two kinds of control in the public sector: internal control and external control.

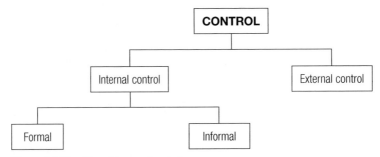

Figure 2.3 The different types of control.

Internal control can be formal or informal. It is usually exercised by those in managerial positions or by other agencies in the executive branch of government. Internal control consists of directing, regulating, supervising, advising, inspecting and evaluating the activities of subordinates.

External control refers to measures that are imposed by government and that affect the operations of an organisation. The table below gives a summary of the two control processes.

INTERNAL CONTROL		EXTERNAL CONTROL
Formal	**Informal**	
Examples include the following: • **Written reports:** they provide practical evidence of what has taken place • **Investigation and inspection:** takes place in the actual work environment.	Examples include the following: • Supervision and leadership	Examples include the following: • Tax laws • Labour laws such as the Basic

INTERNAL CONTROL		EXTERNAL CONTROL
Formal	**Informal**	

Advantages:
 	
  – Findings are easily established and corrective measures can be taken immediately.
 	
Disadvantages:
 	
  – It usually takes place after the activity has been done
  – It may result in negative fault finding if not handled carefully.
 	
• **Auditing:** a systematic examination and verification of books of accounts, records, transactions, documents and physical inspection of assets and inventory of an organisation. It is done by the office of the Auditor-General. The aim of auditing is to:
  – Prevent wrongful and illegal transactions
  – Prevent wasteful expenditure
  – Ensure accountability
  – Encourage efficiency and effective use of resources.
 	
Types of audit:
 	
  – Accounting audit: examines the correct recording of all financial transactions
  – Appropriation audit: examines whether funds are being spent within the financial year in which they are allocated and according to legislation
  – Performance audit: examines whether funds have been used efficiently and economically without being wasteful expenditure.
 	
• Cost accounting, cost comparisons and cost analysis
  – Standard transactions are evaluated at the operational level
  – Control is exercised before a project is approved and implemented
  – Cost comparison is used where many organisational units provide similar goods and services.
 	
• Statistical returns
  – Can be used to measure productivity
  – Figures reflecting costs can be used together with other statistical returns to provide a method for assessing results and for compiling work programmes involving the allocation of personnel and resources.
	• Emphasising a sense of duty, willingness to work, diligence, national pride, self-development and professional pride and integrity.
	• Emphasis on morale and *esprit de corps* (feeling of devotion and pride in the group to which one belongs).
		Conditions of Employment Act, No. 75 of 1997, which gives effect to the right to fair labour practices.

Key point: Control helps to ensure that those in public offices are held accountable for their actions and decisions.

Power break 2.3   INDIVIDUAL WORK

In this unit you learned that control helps to ensure that those in public offices are held accountable for their actions and decisions.

1 Discuss the steps that your community has taken to control the actions and decisions of public officials in your local municipality.
2 Do you think the steps were helpful? Give reasons for your answers.

UNIT 2.4 **The control process**

The **control process** derives from the goals and strategic plans of the organisation. It involves carefully collecting information about a system, process, person or group of people in order to make necessary decisions about them. Basically, the control process consists of four key steps.

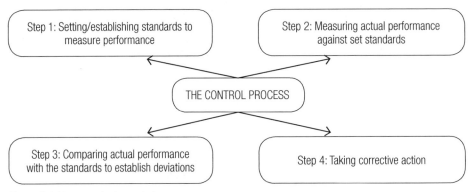

Figure 2.4 Key steps in the control process.

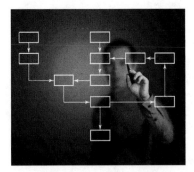

Figure 2.5 The control process has certain steps that need to be followed.

DEFINITION

control process – a system where standards are set against which performance is measured, and corrective action is taken when deviations occur

---

Setting standards to measure performance

Standards refer to definite criteria against which results are measured. They are established by management as a rule for the measurement of the following:

- Quantity: concerns the amount; how much can be produced in a given time. For example, the number of requests that can be processed in one hour
- Quality: concerns the results that can be observed. For example, the time taken by a client waiting in a bank before he/she is served can be used to determine the quality of service rendered by the bank.

Example 2

If you went to a mechanic to have your car serviced, the mechanic's company might ask you to rate their service afterwards. If you waited a long time to get your car back, or the communication was poor or unfriendly, you might give them a bad rating and they would know that the quality of the service was bad.

Figure 2.6 Customers can provide feedback on the quality of the service they receive.

When setting standards, it is important to know the purpose for which they are required. The following are some of the purposes for which standards are set:

- **Time:** standards are set according to the time that is required to complete a task
- **Cost:** standards are set according to the expenditure required to produce a product
- **Income:** standards are set according to rewards that can be received after completing a task
- **Productivity:** standards are set to measure how much can be produced per man hour.

Standards must meet the following requirements:

- All those who are affected by the standards must first accept them
- Standards must be realised within a given time limit
- Standards must suit the abilities of employees.

Measuring actual performance against set standards

Measurement involves comparing actual performance against set standards. In order to measure performance against the set standards the following instruments are used: written reports, inspection, auditing, statistical reports and daily files. These instruments are discussed in detail on the next page.

- Written reports
  - They are mostly used in government departments and institutions
  - They provide documentary evidence of what exactly transpired
  - They are easy to keep
  - They are an effective means of communication
  - They are a permanent record and can be used as a source of reference.
- Inspection
  - It is carried out by supervisors
  - It takes place at the workplace
  - It can be formal or informal
  - It usually takes place after the task is done.

Figure 2.7 Written reports are often used in government departments and institutions.

- Auditing
  - Auditing in public institutions is carried by the office of the Auditor-General
  - It takes place after the task or transaction has taken place
  - It helps to ensure correctness of transactions.
- Statistical reports
  - They are used in addition to financial auditing.
- Daily files
  - They are used to see whether templates, letters and correspondence comply with the requirements of the department.

Comparing actual performance with the standards to establish any deviations

When comparing the actual performance against set standards the following must be checked:

- **Was the actual performance above the set standard?** This could be due to the following: low standards had been set, improved technology or better procedures and methods were used.
- **Was the actual performance equal to the set standard?** This could be due to the following: capacity of the department was not fully utilised and steps should be taken to improve performance.
- **Was the actual performance below the set standard?** This could be due to the following: set standards were too high, events, such as strikes, in the department could have disturbed progress.

Taking corrective action

Corrective action can be determined by assessing the cause and nature of deviations. The following corrective actions can be taken:

- Adjusting the set standards
- Correcting the shortcomings that caused deviations in performance
- Getting approval of employees when correcting matters that caused deviations.

> **Key point:** The control process consists of the following four steps: setting standards, measuring performance against the set standards, establishing deviations and taking corrective action.

Power break 2.4 CLASS DISCUSSION

You want to improve teaching and learning in your class.

1 Discuss the standards you can set to improve teaching and learning.
2 Discuss how the process of teaching and learning can be measured against the set standards.
3 What corrective actions can be taken to improve teaching and learning in your class?

UNIT 2.5 **Public accountability**

The concept of accountability has become the cornerstone of public administration in modern democratic governments. In Unit 2.1 we defined accountability. In this unit, you will learn about **public accountability**. Public accountability refers to the relationship between government and the public where government officials must be answerable for their actions, omissions, decisions and policies. Accountability in South Africa is

Figure 2.8 Residents protest against a lack of service delivery in Phillipi, Western Cape.

usually considered through the points of view of the legislative authority, courts of justice and the public media. These aspects are discussed in detail on the next page.

> **DEFINITION**
>
> **public accountability** – when government is answerable to the citizens for its actions, decisions and policies

Accountability by the legislative authority

The legislature (Parliament) is a body of elected people who represent the voters in different constituencies. The elected officials, or Members of Parliament (MPs) as they are called, are accountable to the public (voters). In order for the MPs to give proper account to the public, they play an oversight role on the activities of government. By overseeing the activities of government, Parliament ensures that service delivery takes place. When exercising oversight, Parliament focuses on the following areas:

- Implementation of laws
- Application of budgets
- Strict observance of laws of Parliament and the Constitution
- Effective management of government departments.

There are many reasons why the oversight role of Parliament is important in South Africa. They include the following:

- To detect and prevent abuse
- To prevent illegal and unconstitutional conduct of government officials
- To protect the rights and liberties of citizens
- To hold government answerable for how taxpayers' money is spent
- To make government operations more transparent and to increase public trust in the government.

Oversight is a function granted by the Constitution to legislative authorities at all government levels to monitor and oversee government actions. Accountability by the legislative authority is provided by the Constitution as follows:

1. Section 89 of the Constitution provides that Parliament can remove or impeach the President on the grounds of:
   - A serious violation of the Constitution or the law (violation of the Oath of Office to uphold the Constitution)
   - Serious misconduct
   - Inability to perform the functions of the office.
2. Section 92 of the Constitution provides that members of the cabinet or ministers are accountable, collectively and individually, to Parliament for the exercise of their powers and the performance of their functions. They must:
   - Act in accordance with the Constitution
   - Provide Parliament with full and regular reports concerning matters under their control.
3. Section 141 (1)(2) of the Constitution provides that a majority of the members of the provincial legislature can pass a vote of no confidence in the Provincial Executive Council or the Premier respectively.

4. Section 133 of the Constitution provides that members of the Executive Council of a province are accountable, collectively or individually, to the provincial legislature for the exercise of their powers and the performance of their functions. They must:
    –   Act in accordance with both the provincial Constitution and the national Constitution.
    –   Provide the legislature with full and regular reports concerning matters under their control.

Case study

Zuma: "I don't know the reasons for Grace Mugabe's exit."

10 January 2018

Figure 2.9 President Jacob Zuma.

Opposition parties wanted President Jacob Zuma to account in Parliament why the Zimbabwean first lady, Grace Mugabe, was granted diplomatic immunity after she had assaulted a South African citizen.

The president responded that he was not a lawyer and was not involved in the process that led to the granting of diplomatic immunity to Zimbabwe's first lady. He argued that the police were actively involved in dealing with the matter and that he did not know the reasons for the granting of immunity to Grace Mugabe.

Zimbabwe's first lady, Grace Mugabe, had come to South Africa where she assaulted a South African lady whom she had seen with her sons. She was not on a diplomatic mission when the incident occurred. The government of South Africa granted her diplomatic immunity so that she could leave the country without any criminal charges laid against her.

Questions

1   Why do you think Zimbabwe's first lady, Grace Mugabe, was granted diplomatic immunity after she had assaulted a South African citizen?
2   Do you believe that President Jacob Zuma did not know why Grace Mugabe was given diplomatic immunity?
3   Why do you think the President had to explain in Parliament why Grace Mugabe received diplomatic immunity?
4   If you were the president of South Africa, how would you have handled Grace Mugabe's case?

Accountability of courts of justice

The courts of justice in South Africa constitute the judicial system of the country. The judiciary is the name given to the body of judges and magistrates who sit in the courts of law. The courts are independent and subject only to the Constitution and the law. They must function impartially, without fear, favour or prejudice. An order or decision issued by a court is binding on all the people, institutions, organisations and organs of state to which it applies.

Accountability of the courts of justice can be explained as follows:

- Court hearings are open to the public. This is necessary in order to avoid suspicions of corruption and possible unfair court verdicts.
- Court hearings or cases can be reported in the media to ensure publicity. When people know that their cases will be published, they try to avoid ending up in court.
- Aggrieved citizens can file a case if their rights are violated. The courts cannot deny the rights of individuals to file cases with them if they are aggrieved.
- The courts have the authority and right to examine the legality and validity of acts of executive institutions in order to protect the rights of citizens.
- Courts can point out the guilty party, however, they are not able to correct or change the behaviour of people.

Figure 2.10 The courts examine legal matters in order to protect citizens' rights.

Accountability by the public media

Public media refers to how communication with the public takes place. They include television, radio, magazines, journals and newspapers. Public media enable government to communicate important information to the public, and they allow members of the public to communicate with government. It is therefore important for public media to be objective and to base their reporting on facts and accurate information rather than being biased.

Accountability by the public media can be explained as follows:

- They hold political and executive officials and **public institutions** accountable for their actions by providing forums for debate and discussions

> **DEFINITION**
>
> **public institutions** – the institutions that are owned or run by government; also known as government institutions

- They spread public policies and public views about different aspects that affect people's lives
- They connect the views of the public with those of government
- They report important issues that take place in government to the public.

For example, in the Case study below, we can see how the media informs the public about important issues. The media reported the violent behaviour of the Deputy Minister of Higher Education and Training. The minister

Figure 2.11 Types of public media.

responded through the media and the media reported the minister's resignation. It is possible that without the media the case of the minister could not have been given much publicity and the minister may not have resigned.

Case study

BREAKING NEWS: Deputy Minister Manana resigns

News at Ten reported that the Deputy Minister of Higher Education and Training, Mr Mduduzi Manana had resigned after he had assaulted two women at the Cubana nightclub in Fourways, Johannesburg.

Questions

1 Which media source reported the case of the Deputy Minister of Higher Education and Training?
2 Why do you think the deputy minister resigned from his position?
3 What role do you think the media played in this case?
4 Why do you think the media is important to both the public and public officials?

Key points:

- Public officials are accountable to the public (voters) and in public.
- Public accountability refers to the relationship between government and the public where government officials must be answerable for their actions, omissions, decisions and policies.

Gigaba dodges accountability on Guptas' citizenship

1 August 2017

The Finance Minister of South Africa, Mr Malusi Gigaba, is said to have avoided accountability on the naturalisation of some members of the Gupta family. Mr Gigaba and his successor as Minister of Home Affairs, Hlengiwe Mkhize, were due to appear before the portfolio committee on Home Affairs.

Mr Gigaba informed the committee that he could not attend the meeting due to "prior commitments"

Figure 2.12 Finance Minister, Malusi Gigaba.

and Ms Mkhize also could not attend because she was out of the country. At the same time, the acting minister of Home Affairs, Ms Faith Muthambi, could also not attend the meeting due to "prior commitments". The opposition MPs were not impressed by the failure of Mr Gigaba to attend the portfolio committee meeting. They argued that the executive should respect the decisions of Parliament and that they should be accountable for their actions as required by the Constitution.

However, the meeting continued with the director-general of Home Affairs, Mkuseli Apleni, who outlined the process of naturalisation to the committee. Mr Gigaba later wrote to argue that the process of naturalisation of some of the members of the Gupta family was done "by the book" although it was never tabled in Parliament as required by law.

Questions

1 According to the passage, who was the Finance Minister at the time this article was published?
2 Why did Mr Gigaba not attend the meeting?
3 What was the purpose of the meeting?
4 Discuss why you think members of the executive must be accountable for their actions and decisions.
5 Based on your knowledge of naturalisation from N4, what is naturalisation and who is responsible for the naturalisation of foreign nationals in South Africa?
6 Why do you think Mr Gigaba refused to account for the naturalisation of some of the members of the Gupta family?
7 What do you think is the role of Parliament in the naturalisation of foreign nationals?
8 Discuss why you think the oversight role of Parliament is important?

UNIT 2.6 The Public Protector (ombudsman)

The office of the **Public Protector** is one of the Chapter 9 institutions in South Africa. Chapter 9 institutions are established in terms of Chapter 9 of the South African Constitution, 1996. The purpose of Chapter 9 institutions is to guard and support constitutional democracy in the country.

DUBLIC DROTECTOR SOUTH AFRICA

**Accountability • Integrity • Responsiveness
Justice • Good Governance**

Figure 2.13 The logo of South Africa's Public Protector.

Appointment and qualification of the Public Protector

The Public Protector is appointed by the President on the recommendation of the National Assembly, in terms of Chapter 9 of the Constitution, 1996. The term of office of the Public Protector is a non-renewable period of seven years. To qualify as Public Protector, one must be a South African citizen who is suitably qualified and experienced and has exhibited a reputation for honesty and integrity.

Powers and functions of the Public Protector

The powers and functions of the Public Protector are regulated by national legislation and are found in Section 182 of the Constitution. The Public Protector has the power to:

- Investigate any conduct in state affairs or in the public administration in any sphere of government that is alleged or suspected to be improper or to result in any impropriety or prejudice and to report on that conduct and to take appropriate remedial action
- Protect citizens from abuse by political and public officials
- Make sure that legislative and executive authorities do not exert power unfairly over the voter
- Investigate abuse of power, violations of human rights, maladministration, mismanagement and dishonesty with regards to public money for self-enrichment
- To recommend corrective actions and issue reports
- Summon people to give evidence under oath when necessary
- Bring any matter to Parliament so that it can be debated

> **DEFINITION**
>
> **Public Protector (ombudsman)** – an official who is appointed by government to investigate complaints made by the public against government agencies or officials

Specific matters that can be investigated by the Public Protector include, but are not limited to, the following:

- Undue delay, for example undue delay in processing a passport or birth certificate
- Improper enrichment, especially using public funds to enrich oneself
- Abuse of power by public officials
- Improper conduct of public officials
- Maladministration in government institutions
- Human rights violations.

Key points:

- No person, institution or organ of state may interfere with the functioning of the office of the Public Protector.
- The Public Protector is subject only to the Constitution and the law, and is independent of government and any political party.

Did you know?

- The Public Protector may not investigate decisions reached by the court.
- The Public Protector must be accessible to all persons and communities.

Power break 2.5 GROUP WORK

1 Explain the powers and functions of the Public Protector.
2 Discuss why you think the office of the Public Protector is important in holding the executive to account for their actions and decisions. Give relevant examples.
3 The former Public Protector, Thuli Madonsela, reported on the issue of state capture. Why do you think the state capture report was necessary?

WHAT DO WE KNOW AND WHERE TO NEXT...

Revisiting the learning objectives

Now that you have worked your way through this module, let's see if you have achieved the learning objectives that we set out at the beginning. In the table that follows we summarise the main concepts that you should know for each learning objective.

Learning objectives	What you have learned
Describe the specific nature of state control	Control helps to detect and regulate undesirable activities such as theft, corruption and delay in work and unco-operative attitudes.
	It is important to exercise control over executive institutions because:
	• Public institutions are established by government to meet the needs, demands and requirements of the public. In this way, government maintains its control over policy, financing, organising, procedures and management of public purposes.
	• Funds made available by Parliament are public funds that are kept in trust until they are spent for specific purposes that benefit the public. The use of public funds must be controlled to minimise unethical behaviour such as theft, bribery, corruption, nepotism and wastage.
	• Control must be exercised over actions and decisions of public officials to ensure legitimacy and legality.
	• The objectives of government include maintenance of law and order, welfare and peace. Control helps to ensure that the objectives of government are maintained.
Explain the kinds of control for public institutions	Kinds of control for public institutions include the following:
	• **Internal control,** which is usually exercised by those in managerial positions or by other agencies in the executive branch of government. It consists of directing, regulating, supervising, advising, inspecting and evaluating the activities of subordinates.
	• Internal control can be **formal** or **informal.**
	• Formal control includes:
	– Written reports
	– Investigation and inspection
	– Auditing
	– Cost accounting, cost comparisons and cost analysis
	– Statistical returns.
	• Informal control includes:
	– Supervision and leadership
	– Emphasising a sense of duty, willingness to work, diligence, national pride, self-development and professional pride and integrity
	– Emphasis on morale and *esprit de corps* (feeling of devotion and pride in the group to which one belongs)

Learning objectives	What you have learned
Describe the steps in the control process	Steps in the control process include: • Setting or establishing standards to measure performance • Measuring actual performance against set standards • Comparing actual performance with the standards to establish any deviations • Taking corrective action.
Explain the character and manner of public accountability	Character and manner of public accountability: • Accountability by the legislative authority • Accountability by courts of justice • Accountability by the public media.
Explain the nature and use of the Public Protector (ombudsman)	The Public Protector has power to: • Investigate any conduct in state affairs or in the public administration in any sphere of government, that is alleged or suspected to be improper or to result in any impropriety or prejudice and to report on that conduct and to take appropriate remedial action • Protect citizens from abuse by political and public officials • Make sure that legislative and executive authorities do not exert power unfairly over the voter • Investigate abuse of power, violations of human rights, maladministration, mismanagement and dishonesty with regards to public money for self-enrichment • Recommend corrective actions and issue reports • Summon people to give evidence under oath when necessary • Bring any matter to Parliament so that it can be debated.

Assessment

True or false questions

Indicate whether the following statements are TRUE or FALSE. Write only "true" or "false" next to the correct question number.

1. Improving the systems of control and accountability in the public sector helps to maintain integrity.
2. The Public Protector is subject only to the Constitution and the President, and is independent of government and any political party.
3. The Constitution supports the concepts of control and accountability.
4. The Public Protector may not investigate decisions reached by the court.
5. It is possible for public officials to be responsible without being accountable.
6. Oversight is a function granted by the Constitution to legislative authorities at all government levels to monitor and oversee government actions.
7. When setting standards, it is important to know the purpose for which they are required.
8. Public accountability refers to the relationship between government and the public where government officials must be answerable for their actions, omissions, decisions and policies.
9. The process of ensuring that actual activities, actions or behaviours conform to set standards and procedures is called accountability.
10. Internal control consists of directing, regulating, supervising, advising, inspecting and evaluating the activities of subordinates.

(10 × 2) [20]

Fill in the missing word or phrase

Write down the correct word or phrase to fill the gaps in the following statements.

1. The _____ protects citizens from abuse by political and public officials.
2. Taking corrective action is a _____ process.
3. _____ refers to definite criteria against which results are measured.
4. _____ is the process of ensuring that actual activities, actions or behaviour conform to set standards and procedures.
5. _____ refers to the relationship between government and the public where government officials must be answerable for their actions, omissions, decisions and policies.
6. _____ is a body of elected people who represent the voters in different constituencies.
7. The courts of justice in South Africa constitute the _____ of the country.
8. _____ consists of the following four steps: setting standards, measuring performance against the set standards, establishing deviations and taking corrective action.

(8 × 2) [16]

Definitions

Define the following terms:

1. Public accountability
2. Control
3. Accountability
4. Auditing
5. Legislature

(5 × 2) [10]

Match the column

Match the term in Column A to the correct description in Column B.

Column A		Column B	
1.	Internal control	A.	Recommends corrective actions and issues reports
2.	Written reports	B.	Takes place within government departments and institutions
3.	Statistical returns	C.	Involves giving an explanation as to why certain activities were done or not done
4.	Public Protector	D.	Can be used to measure productivity
5.	Giving account	E.	The term of office is five years
		F.	Provide documentary evidence

(5 × 2) [10]

Short questions

1. List four steps of the control process. (8)
2. Name five specific matters that the Public Protector can investigate. (10)
3. Explain three conditions on which the president can be impeached. (6)
4. Name the three conditions that must be checked when comparing set standards with actual performance. (6)

Long questions

1. Discuss accountability under the following headings:
   a) Accountability by the legislature
   b) Accountability by the court of justice
   c) Accountability by the public media. (18)
2. Describe the specific nature of state control. (12)
3. Name and explain formal control measures found in the public sector. (20)
4. Discuss the role of the Public Protector. (14)

Grand total: 150

MANAGEMENT FUNCTIONS

This module covers the following aspects of management functions:

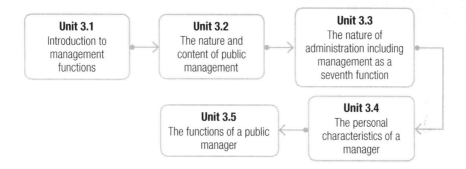

Unit 3.1
Introduction to management functions

Unit 3.2
The nature and content of public management

Unit 3.3
The nature of administration including management as a seventh function

Unit 3.5
The functions of a public manager

Unit 3.4
The personal characteristics of a manager

Learning objectives

After completing this module, you should be able to do the following:
- Take note of the background to management functions
- Explain briefly the nature and content of public management
- Describe briefly the nature of administration, including management as seventh function
- Define the personal characteristics of a manager thoroughly
- Describe the functions of a public manager.

Key terms

administration   manager   public management
government institutions

Starting point

Figure 3.1 Jabulani starting his new role as Director-General at the DHET.

Jabulani has just been appointed the new Director-General (DG) at the Department of Higher Education and Training (DHET). He understands that the purpose of the DHET is to provide educational services to the public. As a DG he has to acquaint himself with the various management functions of the DHET. He has to understand the various management functions that take place in the DHET. In order for him to be effective, he has to plan and organise his department into a number of operational areas. He has to realise that he is now part of management and will also be responsible for directing, co-ordinating and controlling the activities of the employees at the DHET.

Jabulani understands that he is now involved in public administration and public policy. He knows that public administration is concerned with the provision of goods and services to the people. It constitutes the activities and functions that take place within government departments and institutions. DHET is one of the many government departments through which services are provided. A variety of functions need to be performed to meet the needs of the public.

In this module we focus on management functions that take place in the public sector.

UNIT 3.1 Introduction to management functions

In Module 1 you were introduced to generic administrative and management functions. Do you still remember them? Generic administrative and management functions include the following: policy-making, organising, financing, staffing, determination of work procedures and control. In this unit, we revisit the management functions as they take place in government institutions and departments.

Management refers to the process of reaching organisational goals by working with and through people and other organisational resources. The main objective of management is to improve efficiency and effectiveness and to achieve the goals of the organisation. The characteristics of management usually include the following:

- It is a continuous process
- It aims to reach organisational goals
- It is multidimensional
- It is a group activity
- It is a dynamic process.

In the public sector, management functions aim to improve service delivery. It is the responsibility of government officials who work in the various government departments and institutions to ensure good management and improved service delivery. Management functions in government departments are closely related to the purpose for which the department exists.

Example 1

Management functions of the officials at the Reserve Bank of South Africa will help to ensure that the following activities are taking place:

- Formulating and implementing monetary policy for South Africa
- Providing liquidity to banks during periods of temporary cash shortages
- Acting as the banker of other banks
- Helping to settle interbank claims
- Supervising and regulating the activities of other banks in the country.

South African Reserve Bank

Figure 3.2 The logo of the South African Reserve Bank.

Power break 3.1 GROUP WORK

In your groups, discuss the functions of your campus manager. Which of the functions of your campus manager do you consider to be management functions?

UNIT 3.2 The nature and content of public management

Public management takes place in the public sector. Management can be defined as a systematic way of managing people and resources within an organisation to achieve organisational goals. Public management involves the following intellectual functions:

Planning
- Involves choosing the actions that must be carried out to achieve the goals of the organisation.
- Requires the manager to decide what to do and how to do it and to know who will do it well in advance.
- Helps to ensure that both human and other resources are utilised efficiently and effectively.
- Helps to ensure that the organisation is run skilfully and economically.

Organising
- Takes place after planning has been completed.
- Management organises all the necessary resources according to the plan.
- Tasks and responsibilities are assigned to individuals or groups according to their specific skills and competences.
- Management will determine the structure of the organisation (organogram).

Leading/directing
Directing involves the following leadership functions, which are necessary to influence the subordinates to work towards the goals of the organisation:
- Motivation
- Communication
- Guidance
- Counselling
- Regular supervision.

Co-ordinating
- Management is responsible for co-ordinating all the activities of the organisation.
- It involves communication, supervision and giving direction.
- It helps to ensure that all activities function together for the good of the organisation.

> **DEFINITION**
>
> **public management** – a systematic way of managing people and resources within government or public institutions in order to achieve the goals of government

Controlling

- The purpose of control is to ensure that tasks are performed according to set standards
- It is an ongoing process within an organisation
- Control helps management to identify any deviations from set standards and to ensure that corrective measures are taken.

It is important to note that public management is a leadership phenomenon and it is found in all government institutions and departments. Although successful management is a result of team work, organisations usually have one manager who is accountable and who has the final say. He or she makes all the decisions, co-ordinates activities and actions, evaluates results against set standards and takes corrective measures.

Example 2

A college principal at a TVET college makes all decisions, co-ordinates activities, evaluates results and takes corrective action. This ensures that the college runs smoothly, that all the students and staff are happy and productive and that there is a minimum of confusion and indecision.

Figure 3.3 A TVET college principal fulfils a number of responsibilities to do with control.

Management takes place in both the private sector and the public sector. The table below shows the differences between management in the private sector and in the public sector.

Management in the public sector	Management in the private sector
Management decisions are aimed at improving the welfare of the public	Decisions are aimed at maximising profit and are made on behalf of shareholders
Budgets must show balanced spending	Budgets must show growing profits
Applies the provisions of the law	Complies with the provisions of the law
Must use public funds to benefit the public	Must use capital or shareholders or must raise own capital
Decisions are directed by the chief political authority	Decisions are directed by the market

Management styles

Management is based on different management styles. They include the following:

Conformism
This is a management style where traditional practices and standards are followed.
- The manager acts strictly according to the provisions of the law and its regulations.
- No deviations are tolerated or accepted.
- Examples where deviations are not tolerated include police stations, revenue offices and magistrates' offices.

Determinism
This is a management style where all events are determined by causes outside of the human will.
- The manager believes that the fate of their subordinates is predetermined.
- He/she does not consider other people's views.
- He/she must lead his/her subordinates to new heights.
- He/she has a strong belief that what they are doing is correct and is in the best interest of their subordinates.

Dialecticism
This is a management style where differences between two opinions are resolved through reasoning.
- The manager believes in continuous discussion with his/her subordinates.
- He/she undertakes consultative processes.

Figure 3.4 Dialecticism is a management style where differences in opinion are resolved by reasoning.

Did you know?

- To achieve effective planning, managers must gather enough information, exchange ideas with clients and subordinates and make informed decisions.
- An organisational structure helps the organisation to run smoothly.
- Highly motivated employees are likely to be more productive than those who are demotivated.

Key point: Motivation directs the behaviour of employees and stimulates them to work to the best of their ability.

Power break 3.2 INDIVIDUAL WORK

1 In your own words, define public management.
2 If you were the campus manager at your college, how would you motivate your lecturers to perform better?

UNIT 3.3 The nature of administration including management as a seventh function

Public management is an essential element of the administrative function because:

- Decisions made by management are usually guided by policy that came into being because of the process of policy-making (an administrative function). For example, college policies are made following the administrative function of policy-making and all the other management functions are guided by policy.
- It helps to facilitate the direction of activities in the organisation.
- Government institutions and departments cannot operate efficiently without all the seven administrative functions, including public management.

Administration can be defined as a systematic process or activity of running a business or an organisation. Administration takes place in both the public sector and the private sector. In this module, we are concerned about the nature of administration in the public sector. Administration in the public sector refers to the administration of government institutions and departments such as the administration of hospitals, schools, colleges and universities. It consists of the following administrative processes:

- Policy-making
- Organising
- Financing
- Staffing/personnel provision
- Determining work procedure
- Control

DEFINITION

administration – the systematic process or activity of running a business or an organisation

Policy-making

Government institutions and departments require policy that will guide their operations. Policies need to be created. Policy-making is an act of creating laws or setting standards. It involves the following steps:

- Identifying the problem that might be affecting a community, for example, the drought problem in the Western Cape
- Setting an agenda to discuss the problem
- Formulating policy that will help to address the problem
- Adopting the policy by all the stake holders
- Implementing the policy
- Evaluating the policy.

Organising

In order to be effective and to work harmoniously, government institutions and departments need to be properly organised. Organising refers to the way in which the work of a group of people is arranged and distributed among group members within specific structures. It includes the following processes:

- Identifying the activities that need to be performed
- Grouping the activities according to their purpose
- Creating positions and assigning responsibilities for the positions
- Granting authority to those who are assigned responsibilities
- Establishing relationships among the various parts of the organisation to enable people to work together effectively.

Financing

To be implemented, government programmes require a lot of money. Without adequate funding, service delivery will be affected. It is not possible for government to provide services such as education, health facilities and transport and to develop good infrastructure without adequate finance.

City of Cape Town to reallocate funds for water projects

12 January 2018

Finance Minister Malusi Gigaba has given the go-ahead for the City of Cape Town to adjust its budget to be able to fund its water projects aimed at addressing water shortages.

On Monday, the city said Gigaba had finally given Cape Town the green light to reallocate money from its current budget to fund the critical water projects. The city has not indicated how much they plan to reallocate for water projects.

Cape Town is currently at risk of running out of water due to the worst drought in 100 years, and it is running out of time to kick start its water augmentation projects.

The projects include desalination, water reuse and groundwater abstraction, which the city hopes will yield an extra 500 million litres a day.

The City of Cape Town found itself in a difficult situation after Gigaba failed to reply to its requests to make the adjustments. However, in a statement in late October 2017 mayor Patricia De Lille said Gigaba had finally given her administration the thumbs-up.

"The go-ahead from the minister allows me as executive mayor to immediately incur and approve unforeseen and unavoidable expenditure in terms of the [Municipal Finance Management Act]," said De Lille.

She said the green light meant the city no longer had to call a special council meeting to ask for the adjustments to be approved.

Figure 3.5 The city of Cape Town

"I want to thank Minister Gigaba for responding as this will assist us in speeding up the procurement process," said De Lille.

Last week, during her speech in a full council meeting, De Lille said Gigaba had not replied to her requests, which she made in August 2017.

"My request has not been responded to by the Minister except for officials in Treasury asking for clarity which we gave and in the past two months there have been numerous follow-ups to the Minister's office and an appeal to the Presidency," De Lille said at the time.

In her statement from October 2017, De Lille said water consumption was down to 585 million litres of collective use per day.

"I want to thank you, Cape Town, for all your efforts and for being partners as we adapt to the New Normal. We will not allow a well-run city to run out of water," said De Lille.

She said dam levels were at 38.5%.

Questions

1 According to the Case study, who is the mayor of the City of Cape Town?
2 What do you think is the main problem affecting the City of Cape Town?
3 Name the three water projects the City of Cape Town has embarked on to ease the water crisis.
4 How much water is expected from the three projects?
5 What was the mayor requesting from the Minister of Finance?

Staffing and personnel provision

When positions have been created during the process of organising they must be filled by qualified personnel. The human resources department has the responsibility of providing personnel. The process of personnel provision involves the following:
- Analysing and identifying staffing gaps and surpluses
- Recruiting and appointing suitable candidates
- Developing the appointed candidates.

Determination of work procedures
- Work procedures are guidelines that help employees to follow correct procedures at work
- They involve drafting specific instructions that must be followed by employees
- They are written in the form of manuals, regulations or legislation.

Control

Control helps to ensure the following:
- That political goals set by government are carried out efficiently and effectively
- That the work of employees is not in conflict with the policy of government
- That the work of employees does not deviate from the set standards.

Did you know?

- The legislature is responsible for allocating money to various government departments. This takes place when the legislature approves the annual budget.
- The budget year (fiscal year) for central government, in South Africa, runs from 1 April to 31 March.
- The budget speech is presented in Parliament by the Minister of Finance. It takes place before the budget can be implemented. The budget speech is followed by the budget debate.

Power break 3.3 PAIR WORK

Administrative functions are carried out by different divisions or people in an organisation, a government department or a local municipality. From the list, choose the person or division responsible for the administrative function that is shown in the table below.

- Auditors/managers
- Minister/Director-General
- Management
- Treasury
- Human resource division/ Public Service Commission
- Heads of department/ supervisors/managers

Administration function	Responsible person/division
1. Policy-making	
2. Organising	
3. Financing	
4. Staffing/personnel provision	
5. Determination of work procedures	
6. Control	

UNIT 3.4 **The personal characteristics of a manager**

Good leadership is essential to the success of any organisation. A good **manager** is distinguished by certain personal characteristics. These characteristics usually determine how effective and successful the manager can be. The duties of public managers require them to have a great deal of knowledge, personal qualities and skills that help them to plan and predict the future more successfully.

A manager works with people and manages them. A manager must show desirable personal abilities and characteristics that his/her subordinates can look up to and feel comfortable to associate with. The following are some of the abilities of a good public manager:

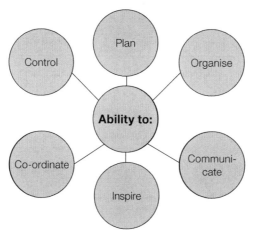

Figure 3.6 The personal characteristics that a manager needs to have.

Ability to plan

Planning is the primary function of a manager. It means deciding in advance what is to be done, when, where, how and by whom. A good public manager must be able to:

- Plan and anticipate possible changes for the future
- Decide matters with sound judgement.

Ability to organise

Organising refers to the way in which the work of a group of people (employees) is arranged and distributed among group members. A good public manager must:

- Be able to organise their subordinates and make them work as a team
- Have thorough knowledge of human nature and be able to work with different people
- Have the ability to communicate.

DEFINITION

manager – a person who is responsible for controlling or administering an organisation or a group of subordinates

---

Ability to communicate

Communication is the process whereby a manager is able to exchange information with his/her subordinates by speaking, using symbols, signs or behaviours. A good public manager must be able to communicate his/her views and opinions meaningfully. He/she must also be able to give the necessary guidance to subordinates through effective communication.

Ability to inspire

- A good public manager must be able to inspire his/her subordinates by caring for them and portraying an enthusiastic and hard-working attitude.
- He/she must encourage them and make them feel confident and eager to work better.
- The performance of employees must not be based on fear of the manager but on inspiration from the manager.

Ability to co-ordinate

Every organisation has certain goals that it aims to achieve. These aims can be achieved if the activities of the organisation are well co-ordinated. Co-ordination is the unification, integration and synchronisation of the efforts of all employees so as to provide unity of purpose within an organisation.

Co-ordination can be achieved by:

- Synchronising activities
- Balancing the workload of employees
- Taking corrective actions to prevent deviation
- Evaluating deviations against set standards.

Figure 3.7 A good public manager can plan carefully in order to get things done whilst balancing the workload of employees.

Ability to control

Control can be defined as the ability to influence or direct people's behaviour. The control process includes:

- Setting meaningful and attainable work and performance standards
- Measuring performance against the set standards
- Evaluating deviations
- Taking corrective action.

A good public manager must also have the following attributes:

- The ability to direct the behaviour of his/her subordinates and the activities of the organisation
- The ability to check, continuously, whether the behaviour of his/her subordinates and the activities of the organisation are still in line with the set standards.
- The ability to acknowledge employees and officials who performed beyond expectation.

Did you know?

- Managers are expected to run their organisations with honesty and integrity.
- Co-ordination is the force that integrates all functions of management in order to achieve organisational goals.
- Management involves planning, organising and co-ordinating, and leadership involves inspiring and motivating subordinates.

Power break 3.4   INDIVIDUAL WORK

1 Based on your knowledge of the characteristics of a good public manager, provide a rating for a campus manager or a principal of a college you have attended. The rating must be for each of the given characteristics in the table below. Use the scale 1 to 5 and tick the appropriate box:

1 = below average, 2 = average, 3 = above average, 4 = good, 5 = very good

Characteristic	1	2	3	4	5
Ability to plan					
Ability to organise					
Ability to communicate					
Ability to inspire					
Ability to co-ordinate					
Ability to control					

2 Based on your choice of the characteristics above, what advice would you give to the manager and why? Discuss your reasons in class.

UNIT 3.5 The functions of a public manager

You have learned that public administration refers to the activities and functions of government that take place in **government institutions** and departments. Government institutions and departments are managed by public managers and public officials who are appointed to work in public offices. They play a critical role in ensuring that the public get the services that they need.

There are three main areas that a public manager must cover. He/she must:

- Attain his/her position
- Determine and establish functions necessary to achieve the objectives of his/her department
- Direct actions, activities and behaviour according to policy.

Once a public manager has attained their position, they need to make sure that they are fulfilling the other functions.

Determine and establish functions necessary to achieve objectives of his/her department

Some of the functions that are necessary for a government department to achieve its objectives include the following:

- Determining and defining aims and policies
- Calculating financial needs
- Determining staff structure and staff needs
- Creating an organisational structure and delegation of functions, authority and responsibilities
- Analysing and revising procedures and methods continuously in the quest for reliable services
- Designing the overall control plans as well as performance levels for individual officials.

Direct actions, activities and behaviour according to policy

Managers must be guided by policy in all their functions. Policy gives them direction in terms of what to do and what not to do. There are three identifiable actions that must be performed by public managers:

- Planning the activities that must be carried out. This involves deciding the activity that has to be carried out, how it should be carried out, when and by whom.

DEFINITION

government institutions – facilities such as TVET colleges, universities or hospitals that are run by government, also known as public institutions

---

- Carrying out the planned activity.
- Controlling how the activity is being carried out. This helps the manager to check if there are any deviations from the set standards.

Apart from the three identifiable actions discussed above, the theory of management consists of various other aspects of management that are important to public managers. They include the following:

- Management is an intellectual process. This means mental plans must be combined with human activity for action.
- Management is directed towards the future, which means planning must be future oriented.
- Management requires constant and careful decision-making. This means there must be thorough reflection on future conditions, facts, data and value judgements.

Figure 3.8 Qualitative and quantitative information (data) is needed in order for management to make good decisions.

- Management has an economic character. This means every administrative and functional action has a financial implication. Actions and decisions must be weighed against their financial implications.
- Management requires social knowledge and experience. Managers must be able to inspire and motivate subordinates to carry out their tasks willingly.
- Management must take place within a framework of political policy directions. Management must make a policy analysis to determine aims and objectives and to plan activities.

- Management requires continuous flow of management information. This is important because information helps managers to assess performance, results, staff abilities, training needs and deviations.
- Management requires continuous evaluation of performance. This enables managers to determine whether employees are doing their tasks correctly or not.

Figure 3.9 Management requires the continuous flow of information in the form of communication. Managers must also be able to help employees who are not doing their tasks correctly.

Did you know? The public sector refers to that portion of an economic system that is controlled by national, provincial or local governments.

Government employs 1.3m public servants

There are almost 1.3 million public servants employed within South Africa's national and provincial governments, Public Service and Administration (PSA), Minister Richard Baloyi said. In a written reply to a parliamentary question, he said national government employed 391 922 people, and the nine provincial governments a total of 891 430 people.

Of the total 1 283 352 government employees, 10 598 were senior managers, 20 996 "middle" managers, and 1 251 758 served at a "non-management service level". Among the provinces, the KwaZulu-Natal government employed the most public servants (187 673), followed by Gauteng (150 303). The Eastern Cape government has 146 714 public servants, while the Western Cape employs 77 820.

Questions

1 According to the Case study, who was the minister of Public Service and Administration in South Africa?
2 According to the Case study, how many senior and middle public managers are employed in South Africa's public service?
3 What are the functions of a public manager?
4 Discuss the characteristics of a good public manager.

WHAT DO WE KNOW AND WHERE TO NEXT...

Revisiting the learning objectives

Now that you have worked your way through this module, let us see if you have achieved the learning objectives that we set out at the beginning. In the table that follows we summarise the concepts that you should know for each learning objective.

Learning objectives	What you have learnt
Take note of the background to management functions	• Management refers to the process of reaching organisational goals by working with and through people and other organisational resources. • The main objective of management is to improve efficiency and effectiveness and to achieve the goals of the organisation. • In the public sector, management functions aim to improve service delivery.

Explain briefly the nature and content of public management	• Public management is regarded as the seventh administrative function.
	• It takes place in the public sector.
	• It involves the following intellectual functions:
	  – Planning
	  – Organising
	  – Leading/directing
	  – Co-ordinating
	  – Controlling.

Describe briefly the nature of administration including management as a seventh function	• Administration can be defined as a systematic process or activity of running a business or an organisation.
	• Administration in the public sector refers to the administration of government institutions and departments such as the administration of hospitals, schools, colleges and universities.
	• It consists of the following administrative processes:
	  – Policy-making
	  – Organising
	  – Financing
	  – Staffing/personnel provision
	  – Determination of work procedures
	  – Control
	  – Public management.
	
	Public management is considered the seventh administrative function because:
	
	• Decisions made by management are usually guided by policy that come into being because of the process of policy-making.
	• It helps to facilitate the direction of activities in the organisation.
	• Government institutions and departments cannot operate efficiently without all the seven administrative functions including public management.

Learning objectives	What you have learnt
Define the personal characteristics of a manager thoroughly	The personal characteristics of a good public manager include the following: • Ability to plan • Ability to organise • Ability to communicate • Ability to inspire • Ability to co-ordinate • Ability to control. A public manager must also have the following attributes: • The ability to direct the behaviour of his/her subordinates and the activities of the organisation • The ability to check, continuously, whether the behaviour of his/her subordinates and the activities of the organisation are still in line with the set standards • The ability to acknowledge employees and officials who perform beyond expectation.

Describe the functions of a public manager	The functions of a public manager cover three main areas:
	
	• Attaining his/her position
	• Determining and establishing functions necessary to achieve objectives of the department
	This is done through the following actions:
	  – Determining and defining aims and policies
	  – Calculating financial needs
	  – Determining staff structure and staff needs
	  – Creating an organisational structure and delegation functions, authority and responsibilities
	  – Analysing and revising procedures and methods continuously in the quest for reliable services
	  – Designing the overall control plans as well as performance levels for individual officials.
	• Directing actions, activities and behaviour according to policy.
	This is done through the following actions:
	  – Planning the activities which must be carried out
	  – Carrying out the planned activity
	  – Controlling how the activity is being carried out.

Assessment

True or false
Indicate whether the following statements are TRUE or FALSE. Write only "true" or "false" next to the correct question number.
1. Anyone who aspires to be a public manager must be involved in active politics.
2. A public manager must be able to anticipate the future.
3. Control is the ability to influence or direct people's behaviour.
4. There are many opportunities for illiterate people in the public sector.
5. Organising means grouping activities according to their purpose.
6. Performance of employees must be based on fear of the public manager.
7. Management in the private sector complies with the provisions of the law.
8. Public management is aimed at maximising profit.
9. Organising takes place before planning.
10. Public management only takes place in the private sector.

(10 × 2) [20]

Abbreviations
What do these abbreviations stand for?
1. DHET
2. DG
3. TVET
4. CEO
5. PSA

(5 × 2) [10]

Definitions
Define the following terms:
1. Public management
2. Co-ordination
3. Organising
4. Planning
5. Administration

(5 × 2) [10]

Match the column

Match the term in Column A to the correct description in Column B.

Column A	Column B
1. Public management	A. It can be achieved by synchronising activities
2. Control	B. It is regarded as the seventh management function
3. Co-ordination	C. They form the most important component of an organisation
4. Public managers	D. It helps management to identify any deviations from set standards and to ensure that corrective actions are taken
5. Employees	E. It aims to disintegrate employees
	F. They are expected to run their organisations with honesty and integrity

(5 × 2) [10]

Short questions

1. Public management involves five intellectual functions. Name these functions. (10)
2. Name the seven administrative functions you have learned about in this module. (14)
3. List three management styles. (6)

Discussion questions

1. Explain the personal characteristics of a manager. (20)
2. Discuss the functions of a public manager under the following headings:
   a) Determining and establishing functions necessary to achieve the objectives of the department. (12)
   b) Directing actions, activities and behaviour according to policy. (6)
3. Discuss the three attributes that a public manager must have. (6)
4. Explain why public management should be considered the seventh administrative function. (6)
5. Discuss management styles under the following headings:
   a) Conformism (4)
   b) Determinism (4)
   c) Dialecticism (4)
6. Briefly describe the nature and content of public management. (8)

Grand total: 150

AUXILIARY FUNCTIONS

This module covers the following aspects of auxiliary functions:

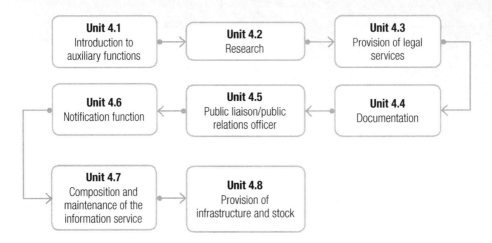

Unit 4.1 Introduction to auxiliary functions → **Unit 4.2** Research → **Unit 4.3** Provision of legal services

Unit 4.6 Notification function ← **Unit 4.5** Public liaison/public relations officer ← **Unit 4.4** Documentation

Unit 4.7 Composition and maintenance of the information service → **Unit 4.8** Provision of infrastructure and stock

Learning objectives

After completing this module, you should be able to do the following:

- Explain the background to and use of auxiliary functions
- Describe research as an auxiliary function
- Explain the provision of legal services as an auxiliary function
- Describe documentation as an auxiliary function
- Describe public liaison as an auxiliary function
- Describe the notification function as an auxiliary function
- Explain the composition and maintenance of the information service as an auxiliary function
- Describe the provision of infrastructure and stock as an auxiliary function.

Key terms

auxiliary functions	infrastructure	research
documentation	legal services	
information services	public liaison	

Starting point

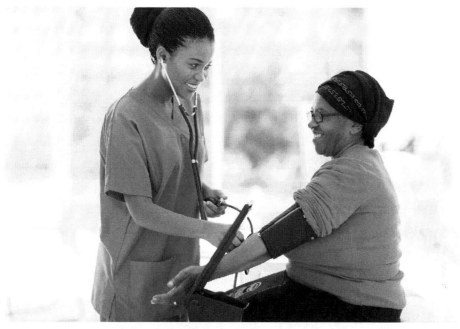

Figure 4.1 Research into medical matters, such as HIV/AIDS research, is an auxiliary function provided by institutions that help government.

South Africa is one of the countries with the highest cases of HIV/AIDS in the world. When so many people are HIV positive the government bears the burden of providing them with the necessary medical services. Government does not always have enough money to provide all the services that are required by the people. Other functionaries are needed to assist government with some of its functions. Functions that are carried out by these institutions are called auxiliary functions or assisting functions.

Do you still remember some of the auxiliary functions you were introduced to in N4? Research institutions usually assist government by conducting research and advising government of their findings.

For example, in 2016 the South African Medical Research Council embarked on research to try and find a cure for HIV. Results of the research are expected towards the end of 2020.

In this module you will learn more about research and other auxiliary functions.

UNIT 4.1 Introduction to auxiliary functions

By now you should be familiar with the generic administrative functions that take place in government departments. You should also know that the purpose of government is to provide services to its citizens. In order to improve the effectiveness and efficiency with which these services are provided, a number of **auxiliary functions** are performed. Some of the auxiliary functions that will be discussed in this module include the following:

- Research
- **Legal services**
- Public relations
- Documentation
- Information services
- **Infrastructure**

In this module you will learn more about the auxiliary functions and how they help to improve efficiency and effectiveness in the delivery of services.

Example 1

Roads are part of a country's infrastructure. They are essential for people and goods to be transported around. The development of roads is an auxiliary function that helps to improve the transportation of goods and services.

Figure 4.2 Building road infrastructure is considered an auxiliary function.

DEFINITIONS

auxiliary functions – extra assistance, especially referring to functions or jobs that the government might not undertake on its own

legal services – the work done by lawyers and the courts

infrastructure – physical facilities such as buildings, pipes, wires, roads and bridges

UNIT 4.2 **Research**

Government aims to improve the lives of its people by carrying out **research** on specific matters. Most government institutions undertake research in their respective functional areas in order to improve efficiency, effectiveness and to save resources. Research institutions usually undertake research on specific matters on behalf of government.

Figure 4.3 Research into specific issues, such as medical research and data analysis, is usually undertaken by research institutions on behalf of govermment.

Flash back to N5: In N5 you learned that research in the public sector is carried out by research institutions that include the following:

* South African Medical Research Council (SAMRC)
* Human Sciences Research Council (HSRC)
* Public Affairs Research Institute (PAR)
* South African AIDS Vaccine Initiative

You also learned that the main function of research institutions is to find innovative and new methods to solve problems that affect communities.

Research can be carried out by parastatal research institutions or by private research enterprises. We will look at each of these research institutions closely.

DEFINITION

research – investigations into the causes of things and how to solve problems

Parastatal research institutions

Parastatal research institutions are research institutions that are either wholly or partially owned by government. They carry out research on behalf of government. Examples of parastatal research institutions include the following:

- National Research Foundation (NRF)
  It was established in 1999 and it has three main functions:
    - To support research and innovation through the agency, Research and Innovation Support and Advancement (RISA)
    - To encourage an interest in science and technology through its business unit, the South African Agency for Science and Technology Advancement (SAASTA)
    - To facilitate high-end research through its National Research Facilities (NRF)
- South African Medical Research Council of South Africa (SAMRC)
    - They are involved in clinical research and public health studies
    - You can read some of the published research papers on their website: http://www.mrc.ac.za/publications/publications.htm
- Agricultural Research Council of South Africa
  It aims to carry out research in order to:
    - Promote agriculture and industry
    - Contribute to a better quality of life
    - Facilitate natural resources conservation
    - Alleviate poverty
- Human Sciences Research Council (HSRC)
    - It focuses on the contribution of science and technology towards poverty reduction, economic development, skills development, job creation and service delivery effectiveness.

Private research enterprises

Unlike parastatal research institutions, private research enterprises operate on their own initiative without assistance from government. They include the following:

- South African Synthetic Oil Liquid (SASOL)
- Anglo American Corporation of South Africa (AACSA)
- Council for Scientific and Industrial Research (CSIR).

> **Did you know?** In 2016 Sasol allocated R15 million to South African universities to conduct strategic research.

> **Key point:** The main function of research institutions is to find innovative and new methods to solve problems that affect communities.

Power break 4.1   PAIR WORK

1   Make a list of four research institutions you learned about in N5.
2   Discuss the kinds of research done by each of the institutions you have listed.

UNIT 4.3 Provision of legal services

Everyone needs some legal services at some point in life. We usually need the services of lawyers or legal advisors when we are dissatisfied with the services rendered or the activities of public officials who work in public institutions. Legal services include the provision of legal assistance to people who cannot afford legal representation and access to the court system. Apart from approaching the courts, the public can also approach the Public Protector when they are dissatisfied with the actions of some public officials.

It is not only individuals who need legal services; public institutions may also need the services of lawyers to advise them on important matters. In order to reduce time and costs, government institutions usually employ their own legal advisors for this purpose. Legal advisors for government are appointed by the Minister of Justice and they must be qualified in the same way as attorneys in the private sector.

> **Did you know?** Members of the public can approach the Public Protector when they are dissatisfied with the services of a government official or a government department.

Government lawyers have the following specific functions:
- They give legal advice to government departments
- They may assist government departments and provincial administrations with the drafting of bills
- They assist with the passage of bills through Parliament
- In civil matters, they give advice to state departments on the interpretation of laws and on the implementation of laws
- They defend government departments and provincial administrations in criminal courts when charges arise from the performance of their official duties.

Figure 4.4 The Constitution of South Africa is the supreme law of South Africa.

> **Key point:** Legal services are auxiliary functions that are central in providing access to justice by ensuring equality before the law, the right to counsel and the right to a fair trial.

Power break 4.2 PAIR WORK

1 List six possible situations in which you think you may need legal services.
2 Discuss your situations or circumstances in pairs.
3 Apart from approaching the courts, the public can also approach the Public Protector when they are dissatisfied with the actions of some public officials. Based on your knowledge of the services of the Public Protector, give five examples of the circumstances under which you can approach the Public Protector.

UNIT 4.4 Documentation

Every day government produces and receives large numbers of documents as it carries out its work. Some of these documents form permanent records for government and are therefore important. Records are important because they provide evidence of actions taken and decisions made by government in its various departments and institutions. Records must be reliable because they contain important information that is needed for the daily function of government. They provide information about who, what, when and why something happened.

Records are kept for various reasons including the following:

- As a source of reference of past transactions in order to perform subsequent actions
- To produce evidence of financial or contractual obligations
- To draw on evidence of past events in order to make informed decisions for the present and the future
- To account for actions and decisions made when required to do so
- To protect individual rights and entitlement
- To safeguard public interest
- To contribute to the historical record of the country.

All government employees have a duty to create full and accurate records of their actions. Government institutions are required to keep records of their activities. Basically, there are two main types of records that need to be kept by public institutions. They include:

Transaction documents
- These include invoices, receipts, payment vouchers and deposit slips.
- They can be kept for a short period before they can be thrown away.

Reference documents
- These are kept by government departments for future use, so they need to be filed in such a way that they can easily be retrieved.
- They include contracts, memorandums, financial records and employment records.
- They must be kept for long periods of time or indefinitely.
- They must be protected against damage or destruction.
- There must be a proper filing system to keep them safe.
- They are usually kept in archives or registries.

Figure 4.5 Records are kept both in hard copy (paper) and electronically.

> **DEFINITION**
>
> **documentation** – records that are used to prove or make something official

Although original documents are usually kept as hard copies for auditing purposes, in order to reduce the cost of keeping them safely, devices and systems are now available for:
- Magnetic storage of documents on tapes or discs prepared by computer
- Photographing of documents to make storage in roll form, microfiche or aperture cards
- Storage of documents on compact discs and external hard drives of computers
- Electronic filing.

Did you know? There have been a number of government security breaches in recent years where a lot of personal and government information has been stolen. Governments are spending a lot of money on ensuring that the information they have is kept safe.

Power break 4.3   GROUP WORK

1 In your groups, discuss why you think it is important to keep documents in electronic devices rather than keeping them as hard copies.
2 Name and discuss the two main types of documents that must be kept by government institutions.

UNIT 4.5 **Public liaison/public relations officer**

Public liaison or public relations is a professional way of maintaining a favourable public image by an organisation or public institution. No institution would want to damage its reputation by destroying its public image. In the public sector, public relations officers are appointed to create, maintain and enhance the reputation of government institutions. A good public image helps to strengthen the credibility of public institutions.

Example 2

If there was a negative story in the newspapers about how a hospital was badly run and the staff were underqualified, nobody would want to go to that hospital. No one would like to visit a hospital when they know that the staff are incompetent, and that it has a poor reputation of helping patients. Without patients a hospital would soon stop running. That is why a public relations officer or public liaison should work hard to maintain the reputation of a hospital, or any other company or institution.

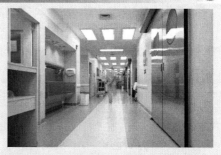

Figure 4.6 Hospitals, just like other institutions, need to maintain a good reputation if they want to continue running effectively.

DEFINITION

public liaison – communication that takes place between officials working together in public institutions

In order to maintain a good public image, public institutions need to:

- Ascertain and evaluate their public image and the attitude of the public with regard to the activities they perform.
- Obtain understanding and acceptance by the public of its objectives and activities.

Public relations officers, or public liaison officers, are expected to be skilled and qualified so that they can promote the image of public institutions in the country. They also act as spokespersons for their institutions and they respond to questions from the media. The liaison or public relations section of public institutions and government departments performs the auxiliary function of public liaison or public relations.

Did you know? The British public relations company Bell Pottinger got into a lot of trouble in 2017 for the work they did in South Africa. Read more about this in the Case study that follows.

Case study

Bell Pottinger apologises for South Africa campaign

The British public relations firm Bell Pottinger is needing to salvage its own reputation regarding work it has done for a South African company owned by the Gupta family. Leaked emails reportedly show that the firm suggested its client doctored its Wikipedia page to present itself in a better light.

Revelations about the PR company's efforts to design a social media campaign which caused racial tensions in South Africa last week prompted Bell Pottinger's chief executive to make a rare apology. The campaign aimed to raise awareness about what was termed "economic apartheid", representing Oakbay, a company owned by the family of Indian businessmen thought to hold the levers of power in Jacob Zuma's government.

Critics say the purpose of the campaign was to deflect attention from allegations of corruption surrounding the South African president, and that by exacerbating racial tensions the PR firm has "left deep scars" in the country's social fabric.

The company has previously represented the Syrian first lady Asma al-Assad; Oscar Pistorius, after he was charged with murder; FW de Klerk, when he ran against Nelson Mandela for president; Alexander Lukashenko, the Belarusian dictator; and the governments of Bahrain and Egypt.

Questions

1 What does the abbreviation PR mean?
2 Which family did the company represent?
3 How many other representations has the company made before?
4 Why did people criticise Bell Pottinger's campaign?
5 Why do you think the company had to apologise?

Power break 4.4 GROUP WORK

In your groups, carry out a debate about why you think public liaison or public relations is an important auxiliary function in public institutions and departments.

One team can take the position that public relations divisions help public institutions to run better by allowing them to focus on their jobs and not on rumours and negative speech about them.

The other team can argue that public relations officers work towards hiding corruption and poor management, and prevent the public from finding out what is really happening.

UNIT 4.6 **Notification function**

Figure 4.7 The City of Cape Town has an SMS service that reminds you when you need to phone in your water meter reading.

The public must always be informed about the activities of government: what the government has done and what it intends to do. Notification services help the public to plan and to hold government accountable for their actions. By notifying the public of its decisions and activities, the government promotes transparency and accountability.

It is the duty of government institutions to inform the public about their activities and decisions. This is because the public:
- Should know what goods and services are available to them,
- Should, for the performance of their "watchdog" function, be informed about the activities of the public institutions
- Should be informed about any purchases that the public institution intends to make so that they can submit tenders
- Can assist government institutions in the performance of their functions.

The government gazette is the official medium of communication that is used by government to inform the public about its activities. It is available at all three levels of government. Government gazettes are published as one of the following:
- National Gazette: Contains information of a legal, administrative and general nature
- Regulation Gazette: Contains information that government wishes to communicate specifically pertaining to regulations only
- Extraordinary Gazette: Contains information that is urgent in nature. It acts as a supplementary edition of the National Gazette and can be published any day of the week.

Information that is published in the government gazette includes the following:
- Proclamations by the President and premiers
- Regulations and notices such as Acts of Parliament, changes of names, financial statements and company registrations
- Decisions made by the President
- Municipal by-laws
- Notices from law societies and notices about the sale of public property.

Power break 4.5   INDIVIDUAL WORK

1. Find a government gazette on the internet or from your local municipality.
2. List any five notices that are published in the gazette.
3. Do you think the public is aware of these notices? Give reasons for your answers.

UNIT 4.7 Composition and maintenance of the information service

Government requires adequate and reliable information in order to provide services. **Information services** include collection, processing and storing of information. The information that is stored can be retrieved when it is required. Information helps the public to know more about their communities or how the government works.

Information in the public sector can be found in two categories:

- Information regarding the operations of government institutions and departments
  For example:
  - How many TVET colleges were built in 2017?
  - How many students received bursary money in 2016?
  - Which college had the highest pass rate in Public Administration in 2016?
  - How many road accidents were recorded during the Easter holiday in 2017?
- Information regarding the administration of government institutions and departments
  For example:
  - What was the decision of government regarding the policy on free education?
  - What steps did the government take to solve the problem of gang violence in the Western Cape?

Information regarding the administration of government requires transparency and accountability. The public would always want to know if promises made by government were fulfilled.

Information is usually used for planning purposes. It must be reliable, factual and adequate. In order to have reliable, factual and adequate information, there must be a system to ensure that:

- The collection, processing and classification of data, the storing of data and retrieving of data is up to standard
- Information collected, processed and stored is in respect of the whole range of activities constituting public administration
- Information stored in an information system can be obtained from statistical returns, books, periodicals, newspapers, files, minutes of meetings and discussions with knowledgeable people
- Information is updated regularly; new data is added and obsolete or outdated data is eliminated.

It is important to know that in the current world of technology, information is usually stored in the hard drive of computers. Traditionally, information was stored in physical files.

> **DEFINITION**
>
> **information services** – services that provide knowledge about something

Power break 4.6 GROUP WORK

1 Visit a police station in your area and collect information about the following:
   • Number of robberies reported in the past three months
   • Number of drunken drivers caught during the past three months
   • Number of people convicted for driving without licences in the past three months
   • Number of road accidents reported during the past three months.
2 Do you think the information you have collected is reliable? Give reasons for your answer.
3 According to the information you collected, which incidents do you think need urgent attention and why?

UNIT 4.8 Provision of infrastructure and stock

Infrastructure development is good for the public. Can you imagine if your college did not have water, electricity or accessible roads, or what if the buildings were not there at all? These are some of the different types of infrastructure that benefit the public. Different types of infrastructure assist government to provide services to the public more efficiently and effectively and in different ways.

Figure 4.8 Pylons are essential infrastructure because they help to carry electricity to our homes.

Examples of the different types of infrastructure can be seen in the table below.

Type of infrastructure	Why it is necessary
Internet and internet services	Enables the public to communicate easily. The internet also helps students when they carry out their research.
Gautrain and rail services	Rail transport helps to reduce congestion on the roads by transporting people and goods in larger quantities.
Universities, colleges and schools	They provide education services to the public.
Hospitals and clinics	The public visit hospitals and clinics when they fall ill.
Power stations	They provide electricity and other forms of energy to the public.

Although every country requires the best form of infrastructure, this is not always possible. There are several factors that will determine the demand for specific infrastructure in a country. Some of the factors that will determine the development of infrastructure in a country include the following:

- Goals of the government of the day
- Ability of the government
- The level of economic development of the country
- Social demand
- Historical development of the country.

In order to function well, infrastructure needs to be maintained continuously. Maintaining infrastructure is very expensive and government needs a lot of money to maintain its existing infrastructure.

Did you know? South Africa developed several stadiums (infrastructure) in order to host the FIFA World Cup in 2010.

Power break 4.7 GROUP WORK

1 Make a list of the different types of infrastructure in your area.
2 In your groups, discuss why each of the types of infrastructure you have listed is important.

WHAT DO WE KNOW AND WHERE TO NEXT...

Revisiting the learning objectives

Now that you have worked your way through this module, let us see if you have achieved the learning objectives that we set out at the beginning. In the table that follows we summarise the concepts that you should know for each learning objective.

Learning objectives	What you have learnt
Explain the background to and use of auxiliary functions	• The purpose of government is to provide services to the public. • Auxiliary functions enable government to improve the effectiveness and efficiency with which it provides services to the public.
Describe research as an auxiliary function	• Government aims to improve the lives of its people by carrying out research on specific matters. • Government institutions undertake research in their respective functional areas in order to improve efficiency, effectiveness and to save resources. • Research institutions usually undertake research on specific matters on behalf of government. • Research can be carried out by parastatal research institutions or by private research enterprises.
Explain the provision of legal services as an auxiliary function	• People need the services of lawyers or legal advice when they are dissatisfied with the services rendered or the activities of public officials. • Legal services include the provision of legal assistance to people who cannot afford legal representation and access to the court system. • The public can also approach the Public Protector when they are dissatisfied with the actions of some public officials. • Public institutions also need the services of lawyers to address certain issues or to advise them on important matters.
Describe documentation as an auxiliary function	• Documents are important because they provide evidence of actions taken and decisions made by government. Documents are kept for the following reasons: • As a source of reference of past transactions in order to perform subsequent actions • To produce evidence of financial or contractual obligations • To draw on evidence of past events in order to make informed decisions for the present and the future • To account for actions and decisions made when required to do so • To protect individual rights and entitlement • To safeguard public interest • To contribute to the historical record of the country.

Learning objectives	What you have learnt
	Two main types of documents that need to be kept are:
	Transaction documents
	• These include invoices, receipts, payment vouchers and deposit slips.
	• They can be kept for a short period before they can be thrown away.
	Reference documents
	• They are kept by government departments for future use, so they need to be filed in such a way that they can easily be retrieved.
	• They include contracts, memorandums, financial records and employment records.
	• They must be kept for long periods of time or indefinitely.
	• They must be protected against damage or destruction.
	• There must be a proper filing system to keep them safe.
	• They are usually kept in archives or registries.
	In order to reduce the cost of keeping documents safely, devices and systems are now available for:
	• Magnetic storage of documents on tapes or discs prepared by computer
	• Photographing of documents to make storage in roll form, microfiche or aperture cards
	• Storage of documents on compact discs and external hard drives of computers
	• Electronic filing systems.
Describe public liaison as an auxiliary function	• Public liaison or public relations is a professional way of maintaining a favourable public image by an organisation or public institution.
	• A good public image helps to strengthen the credibility of public institutions.
	In order to maintain a good public image, public institutions need to:
	• Ascertain and evaluate their public image and the attitude of the public with regard to the activities they perform
	• Obtain understanding and acceptance by the public of its objectives and activities.
	Public liaison/relations officers:
	• Must be skilled and qualified for their job
	• Act as spokespersons for their institutions and respond to questions from the media.
Describe the notification function as an auxiliary function	• The public must always be informed about the activities of government.
	• Notification services help the public to plan and to hold government accountable for their actions.
	• By notifying the public of its decisions and activities, the government promotes transparency and accountability.
	It is the duty of government institutions to inform the public about their activities and decisions. This is because the public:
	• Should know what goods and services are available to them
	• Should, for the performance of their "watchdog" function, be informed about the activities of the public institutions
	• Should be informed about any purchases that the public institution intends to make so that they can submit tenders
	• Can assist government institutions in the performance of their functions.

Learning objectives	What you have learnt
	The government gazette is the official medium of communication that is used by government to inform the public about its activities. Government gazettes are published as one of the following:
• National Gazette: Contains information of a legal, administrative and general nature
• Regulation Gazette: Contains information that government wishes to communicate specifically pertaining to regulations only
• Extraordinary Gazette: Contains information that is about an emergency or urgent in nature. It acts as a supplementary edition of the National Gazette and can be published any day of the week.
Information that is published in the government gazette includes the following:
• Proclamations by the President and premiers
• Regulations and notices such as Acts of Parliament, changes of names, financial statements and company registrations
• Decisions made by the President
• Municipal by-laws
• Notices from law societies and notices about the sale of public property.
Explain the composition and maintenance of the information service as an auxiliary function	• Government requires adequate and reliable information in order to provide services.
• Information services include collection, processing and storing of information.
• The information that is stored can be retrieved when it is required.
• Information helps the public to know more about their communities or how the government works.
Information in the public sector can be found in two categories:
• Information regarding the operations of government institutions and departments.
• Information regarding the administration of government institutions and departments.
Information is usually used for planning purposes.
It must be reliable, factual and adequate.
In order to have reliable, factual and adequate information, there must be a system to ensure that:
• The collection, processing and classification of data, the storing of data and retrieving of data is up to standard
• Information collected, processed and stored is in respect of the whole range of activities constituting public administration
• Information stored in an information system can be obtained from statistical returns, books, periodicals, newspapers, files, minutes of meetings and discussions with knowledgeable people
• Information is updated regularly; new data added and obsolete or outdated data eliminated.
Describe the provision of infrastructure and stock as an auxiliary function	• Different types of infrastructure assist government to provide services to the public more efficiently and effectively and in different ways.
• In order to function well, infrastructure needs to be maintained continuously.
• Maintaining infrastructure is very expensive and government needs a lot of money to maintain its existing infrastructure.
• Several factors affect the ability of government to provide all the necessary infrastructure required by its citizens.

Assessment

True or false
Indicate whether the following statements are TRUE or FALSE. Choose the answer and write only "true" or "false" next to the question number.

1. The TV is the official medium of communication for government.
2. Records are important documents because they provide evidence of actions taken by central government only.
3. Transaction documents are kept for a very long period of time.
4. A good public image helps to strengthen the credibility of public institutions.
5. Notifications help government to promote inefficiency.
6. Members of the public cannot approach the Public Protector for legal advice.
7. The Agricultural Research Council of South Africa aims to alleviate poverty in the country.
8. The National Research Foundation is an example of a private research enterprise.
9. Auxiliary functions help government to improve efficiency and effectiveness.
10. The main function of research institutions is to find innovative and new methods of solving problems affecting communities.

(10 × 2) [20]

Match the columns
Match the term in Column A to the correct description in Column B.

Column A	Column B
1. Public liaison/public relation officers	A. They help to reduce congestion on the roads by transporting people and goods in larger quantities
2. Infrastructure	B. They may assist government departments and provincial administrations with the drafting of bills
3. SASOL	C. Act as spokespersons for their institutions and they respond to questions from the media
4. Government lawyers	D. Must be reliable, factual and adequate
5. Gautrain and rail services	E. Is an example of a private research enterprise
	F. Is an example of an auxiliary function

(5 × 2) [10]

Abbreviations
What do these abbreviations stand for?

1. SASOL
2. RISA
3. HIV
4. SAMRC

5.   HONG
6.   AIDS
7.   PAR
8.   SAASTA
9.   AACSA
10. NRF

(10 × 2) [20]

Short questions

1.   Name five auxiliary functions you have learned about in this module.   (10)
2.   List four parastatal research institutions.   (8)
3.   What must public institutions do in order to maintain a good public image?   (4)
4.   Name the two main types of documents that need to be kept by government.   (4)
5.   Name the factors that will determine the development of infrastructure in South Africa.   (4)

Discussion questions

1.   Name and discuss the two main types of documents that need to be kept by government.   (20)
2.   Discuss the specific functions of government lawyers.   (10)
3.   The government should inform the public about its activities. Why do you think this is necessary?   (8)
4.   Name and explain the government gazettes that are available to the public.   (12)
5.   In order to reduce the cost of keeping documents, some devices and systems are now available. Name and explain these devices and systems.   (6)
6.   Briefly explain notification as an auxiliary function.   (6)
7.   Describe the system that is required in order to have adequate, reliable and factual information.   (8)

Grand total: 150

INSTRUMENTAL FUNCTIONS AND REQUIREMENTS

This module covers the following aspects of instrumental functions and requirements:

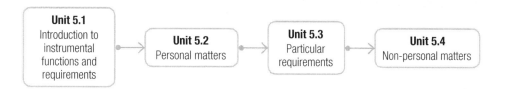

Unit 5.1
Introduction to instrumental functions and requirements

Unit 5.2
Personal matters

Unit 5.3
Particular requirements

Unit 5.4
Non-personal matters

Learning objectives

After completing this module, you should be able to do the following:
- Describe the use and nature of instrumental functions
- Describe communication as an instrumental function
- Explain decision-making as an instrumental function
- Explain offices, workshops, laboratories and other workplaces as an instrumental function
- Describe furniture and equipment as an instrumental function
- Describe motorcar and other transport as an instrumental function
- Describe uniforms and protective wear as an instrumental function
- Describe stationery and similar requirements as an instrumental function.

Key terms

attributes	equipment	stationery
communication	instrumental functions	transport
decision-making	protective wear	work environment

Starting point

Figure 5.1 Farzana did some research to find out why uniforms are necessary in the workplace.

Farzana's cousin works as a paramedic and she has to wear a uniform at work. Farzana wondered why it is necessary to wear uniforms in the workplace. She decided to do a Google search and find out. After a thorough search she discovered that uniforms are important because they enable employees to work better. For example, paramedics need to be recognisable to the public, and mineworkers require helmets, torches, overalls and gumboots to protect them from injury and diseases.

She also learned that uniforms help to distinguish one profession from the other. For example, soldiers and pilots are distinguished by their uniforms and so are police officers. Uniforms and other instruments are always important in the workplace.

In this module, you will learn more about different instrumental requirements, such as uniforms and tools, and why they are important.

UNIT 5.1 Introduction to instrumental functions and requirements

People who work in public institutions such as colleges, universities, hospitals and police stations need to be well trained and competent to carry out their work effectively and efficiently. Each public official is required to carry out personal activities that are important (instrumental) in the performance of their work.

Imagine visiting a college and the official at the front desk is unable to communicate with you, or visiting a hospital where the doctor is unable to make a decision about how to treat your medical condition. The ability to communicate or to make decisions in the **work environment** is an important instrumental requirement that all public officials should meet.

Some instrumental requirements are personal in nature while others are non-personal. Personal matters are associated with the attributes, skills and abilities that people possess while non-personal matters include all the items that will be used by employees to perform their tasks well. Both personal and non-personal matters help employees to work effectively and efficiently. We will learn more about personal and non-personal matters as **instrumental functions** and requirements in Unit 5.2 and Unit 5.4.

Power break 5.1 (GROUP WORK)

1 Visit a local magistrate court in your area during a court session or watch a parliamentary debate on TV. Listen to the proceedings and make some notes about communication in the court room and the decisions made by the magistrate.
2 Based on the notes you made, discuss the importance of communication and the decision of the judge as instrumental functions in court proceedings.
3 What other instruments are used in the court to make court proceedings more effective?

Figure 5.2 Certain instruments are used in court rooms and in Parliament that make communication more effective.

DEFINITIONS

work environment – the conditions in which an employee works or operates

instrumental functions – important skills and abilities that are necessary for one to perform a task

---

Have you ever wondered what makes employees effective in the workplace? Different professions require different types of instruments and tools to enable the employees to work better. For example, those who work in an office need a computer, a chair, a desk, stationery and access to the internet; while nurses put on uniforms and use various medical tools when they are at work. We usually associate different professions with the uniforms they wear or the instruments they use.

Figure 5.3 Office equipment is essential for certain kinds of work.

Some instruments help to protect employees from injury, health risks and other forms of danger. Other instruments are not necessarily for the employee's health or protection, but they are necessary in order to do the job. Imagine if you had to send an email to a colleague at work and you did not have a computer or internet access.

Example 1

Sometimes employees go on strike to demand uniforms and other instruments. In 2016, workers at Matatiele Municipality went on strike demanding protective clothing and uniforms. They accused the municipality of not taking their safety concerns seriously. They demanded gloves, helmets, overalls and masks, which they said the municipality had failed to provide.

UNIT 5.2 **Personal matters**

Most employers seek to hire people who have specific attributes, skills or abilities. These skills and abilities are instrumental to the success of the organisation. Most employers do not want to hire people who do not have the necessary skills or abilities the institution is looking for. The following are some of the abilities that employers look for:

- The ability to communicate
- The ability to work in a team
- The ability to adapt and to make correct decisions
- The willingness to learn.

These **attributes** help employers to choose the right candidates who will promote the goals of the institution. It is important for public institutions to employ people who have the correct attributes for the job.

Figure 5.4 Ability to work in a team is an important attribute in any organisation.

DEFINITION

attributes – characteristics or character traits belonging to certain individuals

Communication

Communication is the act of transferring information from one person to another. In order to communicate, a person needs to be able to make themselves heard and understood, and must also be able to listen to and understand others. The ability to communicate is an important attribute required of employees in both the public sector and the private sector.

A good communicator must also be a good listener. It is important that correct information is communicated in order to avoid confusion and misunderstanding. The success of an organisation depends on the effectiveness and efficiency of its communication system.

Communication can be formal or informal. Formal communication usually follows specific channels (known as communication channels). An example of formal communication would be a company's official handbook. Informal communication, on the other hand, does not need to follow specific channels. An example of informal communication could be a casual discussion between colleagues.

Flashback to N5: In N5 you learned that it is not possible to co-ordinate activities without communicating. Communication can be horizontal or vertical. Horizontal communication takes place between employees working at the same level in an organisation and vertical communication takes place between a superior and a subordinate.

Communication can also be verbal, non-verbal or written. Written communication is usually more formal than verbal or non-verbal communication.

Figure 5.5 Communication can take many different forms.

DEFINITION

communication – the exchange of information by speaking, writing, or using some other medium

Decision-making

Decision-making can be defined as the thought process of selecting the most suitable option out of those available. In order to make a rational decision, the decision-maker must first analyse information, evaluate various alternatives and choose the most favourable option.

When analysing various alternatives, the decision-maker must pay attention to the positive and negative aspects of the alternatives in order to make a rational decision. He or she must also project the possible outcomes of each scenario before selecting the most suitable one for the given situation.

Flashback to N5: In N5 you learned that people make decisions about different things and for different reasons. Important steps in the decision-making process include the following:

1 Analyse the problem
2 Collect data
3 Classify and analyse the data
4 Prepare the data
5 Catalogue alternative solutions
6 Evaluate the alternatives
7 Make the decision
8 Implement the decision
9 Obtain feedback on the effects of the decision.

It is important that we make a distinction between a decision and a policy. A decision can be defined as a choice that is made between various alternative courses of action in order to solve a problem. A policy is the basic principle through which decisions are guided in order to achieve rational outcomes. Decisions are usually made to solve undesirable situations or problems affecting society.

Example 2

A country's government might have a policy of not negotiating with terrorists. If they find themselves in a situation involving terrorists who are making demands, they will need to make the decision about whether or not to enter a discussion with the terrorists. Usually policy will inform decisions, but this does not always happen.

When making decisions the following sequence or steps are usually followed:
- Identify the situation for which a decision must be made
- Decide that something should be done to address the situation
- Make sure that enough information is gathered about the situation
- Decide on various ways to solve the situation
- Make the final decision.

DEFINITION

decision-making – the process of selecting a belief or option from those available

Sometimes final decisions are used to make policy. For example, the attendance policy in TVET colleges is a result of decisions made in order to solve the problem of poor attendance by college students.

Some decisions are programmable while others are not. Programmable decisions are based on facts and are made after sufficient information is gathered. Non-programmable decisions are based on assumptions. They are not supported by sufficient information.

Did you know? The decisions made by government must be guided by policy.

Key point: Before a decision is taken the following specific functions should be performed:

- Examine or observe the situation
- Collect enough information about the situation in order to understand it
- Analyse the information gathered
- Make the final and rational decision.

Power break 5.2 GROUP WORK

South Africa has been experiencing the problem of rhino poaching for a long time. The number of rhinos poached annually has risen from 13 in 2007 to over 1 000 in 2016.

1 In your groups, discuss the problem of rhino poaching in South Africa.
2 Make a list of decisions you would make to combat the problem of rhino poaching in the country.
3 Discuss the advantages and disadvantages of each decision you have listed in question 2.
4 Which one of your decisions would best solve the problem of rhino poaching in South Africa? Give reasons for your answer.

Figure 5.6 Rhino poaching is a major issue in South Africa.

UNIT 5.3 **Particular requirements**

Particular requirements refer to particular skills that are necessary in order for an employee to perform a particular task. For example, it is not possible for anybody to practise as a medical doctor without acquiring certain skills and gaining the necessary qualifications.

In the public sector, the government has to make sure that qualified personnel are hired to perform particular tasks. In order to achieve this, soon after the 1994 elections, the government of the Republic of South Africa had to transform the way the public service is run. The reasons for the transformation of the public service are that:

- Services must be provided impartially, fairly, equitably and without bias.
- People's needs must be responded to.
- The public must be encouraged to participate in policy-making.
- Public administration must be broadly representative of all South Africa people regardless of colour, gender or ethnicity.
- Employment of personnel must be based on ability, objectivity, fairness and the need to redress the imbalances of the past.
- A public service must be provided that is representative, coherent, transparent, efficient, effective, accountable and responsive to the needs of all.

The transformation of the public service requires particular skills that are necessary for the efficient running of the service. This means personnel who are recruited into the service must posses these skills in order to deliver the required services.

Figure 5.7 Specific qualifications are needed in order to become a government employee.

UNIT 5.4 Non-personal matters

In Unit 5.3 you learned that personal matters are associated with the attributes, skills and abilities that people possess. They are necessary to achieve goals of the organisation or institution. In this unit we will learn about non-personal matters. Non- personal matters include all the items that will be used by employees to perform their tasks well. Non-personal matters that will be discussed in this unit include offices, workshops and laboratories; furniture and **equipment**; motorcars and other forms of **transport**; uniforms and protective clothes and stationery.

Different government departments and institutions require different equipment to perform their functions. Some type of equipment is found in all government departments. For example, a government department requires offices, computers and various types of office equipment in order to function effectively and efficiently.

Offices, workshops, laboratories and other workplaces

Can you imagine if your college did not have any classrooms? It would not be possible to get together and learn, and there would be no designated space for your classes. Both learners and lecturers need classrooms to do their work.

Offices, classrooms, workshops, laboratories and other workplaces are found throughout the country and in various communities. They are usually expensive to build. In order to have these workplaces functional, land must be made available, building plans must be made, buildings constructed and maintained. When the buildings are available then the various types of equipment should be bought and used to provide services.

In South Africa, the Department of Public Works is responsible for providing accommodation and property management services to all the other government departments in the country. The functions of the Department of Public Works include the following:

- To buy land for constructing government's accommodation assets
- To meet accommodation requirements for all government departments
- To maintain government buildings
- To hire buildings for use by government departments
- To dispose of government accommodation assets when they are no longer needed.

DEFINITIONS

equipment – items that are used for a particular purpose

transport – the means of moving people or goods from one place to another

Offices, classrooms, workshops, laboratories and other workplaces provide a good working environment that enables government to provide essential services to the public. Employees spend most of their time at work. It is therefore important that they work in a conducive and comfortable environment that enables them to be more efficient, effective and productive.

Figure 5.8 It is important that the workplace is comfortable and conducive to work.

Did you know? The Department of Public Works is the only government department whose mandate is to be the custodian and manager of all national government's fixed assets.

Furniture and equipment

A good working environment is one that has well-organised furniture and equipment. Employees who work in an office with good and well-organised furniture are likely to be more productive than those who work in an environment where the furniture is poorly organised.

Figure 5.9 Furniture and equipment are necessary for employees to do their jobs.

Furniture refers to movable objects such as chairs, tables and desks. The main purpose of furniture is to support human activities. It is important that every workplace has adequate furniture and equipment to enable employees to be more effective, efficient and productive. The following aspects are important with regard to furniture and equipment:

- Furniture and equipment should be acquired easily and at the lowest possible cost
- Furniture and equipment should be protected from theft and damage
- Officials should know how to care for and use the furniture and equipment correctly
- Only suitable furniture and equipment should be acquired for a particular purpose.

> **Key point:** Furniture helps to create a conducive working environment and to increase productivity.

Motorcars and other transport

In most countries government officials do not use public transport, they use government vehicles. In South Africa each government department has their own vehicles that are provided by government.

A fleet manager is usually appointed by government departments to manage the use of government vehicles within the department. Government departments and institutions have appropriate legislation that guides them on the use of government vehicles. Other government departments have put in place specific rules that must be followed when driving a government vehicle.

Motorcars and other forms of transport used by government officials help them to attend to important issues faster. Can you imagine if doctors and nurses were to use public transport to attend to an accident or a patient?

Figure 5.10 Police vehicles allow police personnel to move around quickly.

Some government institutions require that a driver of a government vehicle must undergo specialised training such as defensive driving. When he/she takes the vehicle on a trip the driver must log the following in the logbook:

- The number of kilometres on the odometer
- The time when the vehicle is taken out
- The name and signature of the driver.

Uniforms and protective wear

Employees who work in some government departments and some sections of the private sector are identified by their uniforms. Examples include the following:

- Nurses
- Police officers
- Correctional services officials
- Security guards

Wearing uniforms at work has the following advantages:

- It promotes a sense of team spirit
- Employees have a sense of belonging, for example, the nursing profession, the army and the police
- It improves productivity.

Figure 5.11 Doctors wear uniforms that protect their clothes, make them identifiable and promote a sense of belonging.

DEFINITION

protective wear – clothing that is meant to prevent people from injury when performing a task

Sometimes the work that is done by employees requires them to wear protective clothing. Protective clothing includes hard hats, ear plugs, face masks, respirators and safety glasses.

The Occupational Health and Safety Act, No. 85 of 1993 regulates the use of protective clothing and equipment in South Africa. Protective clothing is essential for some types of jobs. The following types of employees are required by law to wear protective clothing:

- mineworkers
- lab technicians
- cleaners
- groundsmen
- welders.

Figure 5.12 A firefighter wearing protective clothing.

Protective clothing provides safety to employees. It also help to minimise injury due to accidents that may take place at work. Employers are adhering to legislation when their employees wear protective clothing.

Stationery and similar requirements

In order to work productively and efficiently, employees in the public sector require **stationery**. Every public institution requires stationery in order to perform its duties well. Government institutions have to budget for stationery and other necessary requirements for their employees. For example, stationery required by TVET colleges includes: pencils, bond paper, scissors, white board markers, rulers, writing materials, calculators, highlighters, sticky notes and staplers.

Other requirements that are necessary in public institutions are computers and printers. Most TVET colleges require these because they do a lot of typing when they prepare assessments and administer tests.

Power break 5.3   GROUP WORK

1 In your groups, make a list of all the movable equipment at your college.
2 Discuss why each one of the equipment items you have listed helps to improve efficiency and effectiveness.

DEFINITION

stationery – writing materials and office supplies

WHAT DO WE KNOW AND WHERE TO NEXT...

Revisiting the learning objectives

Now that you have worked your way through this module, let's see if you have achieved the learning objectives that were set out at the beginning. In the table that follows we summarise the main concepts that you should know for each learning objective.

Learning objective	What you have learned
Describe the use and nature of instrumental functions	• Instrumental functions help employees to work efficiently and effectively. • Some of the instrumental requirements are personal in nature while others are non-personal. • They help employees to be more productive.
Describe communication as an instrumental function	• Communication is the act of transferring information from one person to another. • Communication helps to minimise misunderstanding. • It is easy to co-ordinate activities at the workplace when there is effective communication. • The success of an organisation depends on the effectiveness and efficiency of its communication system. • Communication can be formal or non-formal, it can also be verbal or non-verbal. • Good communication improves unity of purpose in the organisation.
Explain decision-making as an instrumental function	• Decision-making is the thought process of selecting the most suitable alternative from available options. • It involves analysis of information, evaluation of alternatives and choosing the most favourable alternative. • When analysing the various alternatives, make a rational decision. • The decision-maker must be able to project the possible outcome of each alternative before selecting the most suitable alternative. • Decisions are usually made to solve undesirable situations or problems affecting society. When making decisions the following sequence or steps are usually followed: • Identify the situation for which a decision must be made • Decide that something should be done to address the situation • Make sure that enough information is gathered about the situation • Decide on various ways to solve the situation • Make the final decision.

Learning objective	What you have learned
Explain offices, workshops, laboratories and other workplaces as an instrumental function	• Offices, classrooms, workshops, laboratories and other workplaces are found throughout the country and in various communities. • They are usually expensive to build. • In order to have these workplaces functional, land must be made available, building plans must be made, buildings constructed and maintained. • When the buildings are available then the various types of equipment should be bought and used to provide services. • Offices, workshops, laboratories and other workplaces provide the necessary working environments that enable government to provide essential services. • They also help employees to work more comfortably and to be more efficient and effective.
Describe furniture and equipment as an instrumental function	• Furniture and other equipment plays a vital role in improving the working environment. • A good working environment is one that has well-organised furniture and equipment. • Employees who work in an office with good and well-organised furniture are likely to be more productive than those who work in an environment where the furniture is poorly organised. • The main purpose of furniture is to support human activities. • It is important that every workplace has adequate furniture and equipment to enable employees to be more effective, efficient and productive. The following aspects are important with regard to furniture and equipment: • Furniture and equipment should be acquired easily and at the lowest possible cost. • Furniture and equipment should be protected from theft and damage. • Officials should know how to care for and use the furniture and equipment correctly. • Only suitable furniture and equipment should be acquired for a particular purpose.
Describe motorcars and other transport as an instrumental function	• Government departments use government vehicles to carry out their work. • A fleet manager is usually appointed to manage the use of government vehicles within the department. • The use of government vehicles is regulated by legislation. • Motorcars and other forms of transport used by government officials help them to attend to important issues faster.

Learning objective	What you have learned
Describe uniforms and protective wear as an instrumental function	• Employees who work in some government departments and some sections of the private sector are identified by their uniforms. Wearing uniforms at work has the following advantages: • It promotes a sense of team spirit. • It helps to develop a sense of belonging, for example, within the nursing profession, the army and the police. • It can also improve productivity. Sometimes the work that is done by employees requires them to wear protective clothing. The Occupational Health and Safety Act, No. 85 of 1993 regulates the use of protective clothing and equipment in South Africa. Wearing protective clothing has the following advantages: • It provides safety to employees. • It also helps to minimise injury due to accidents that may take place at work. • The employer is seen to be adhering to legislation when their employees wear protective clothing.
Describe stationery and similar requirements as an instrumental function	• Stationery and similar requirements help employees in the public sector to be more effective, efficient and productive. • Every public institution requires stationery in order to perform its duties well. • Government institutions have to budget for stationery and other necessary requirements for their employees.

Assessment

True or false
Indicate whether the following statements are TRUE or FALSE. Choose the answer and write only "true" or "false" next to the question number.
1. Communication is the act of transferring information from one person to another.
2. The main aim of protective clothing is to be able to identify employees within the working environment.
3. Wearing uniforms helps to promote a sense of unity.
4. Effective communication helps to improve co-ordination activities at the workplace.
5. Instrumental functions help employees to work efficiently and effectively.
6. There is no legislation regarding protective clothing.
7. A fleet manager is usually appointed to manage the use of government vehicles within a government department.
8. The main purpose of furniture is to support human activities.
9. Wearing uniforms does not promote productivity.
10. The use of government vehicles is regulated by legislation.

(10 × 2) [20]

Definitions
Define the following terms:
1. Equipment
2. Decision-making
3. Communication
4. Policy
5. Protective wear

(5 × 2) [10]

Match the column
Match the term in Column A to the correct description in Column B.

Column A		Column B	
1.	Wearing protective clothing	A.	The act of transferring information from one person to another
2.	Wearing uniforms	B.	Involves analysis of information, evaluation of alternatives and choosing the most favourable alternative
3.	Fleet manager	C.	Promotes a sense of team spirit
4.	Decision-making	D.	Takes place in the public sector only
5.	Communication	E.	Is usually appointed to manage the use of government vehicles within the department
		F.	The employer is seen to be adhering to legislation when their employees wear protective clothing

(5 × 2) [10]

Short questions

1. Name four abilities that employers look for when they hire an employee. (8)
2. Define the term "instrumental functions". (4)
3. Explain why it is important to communicate correct information in the workplace. (4)
4. List six ways government departments can communicate with clients outside their department. (12)
5. Discuss the advantages of written communication. (6)
6. Explain the main purpose of furniture at the workplace. (2)
7. Give four examples of stationery used in TVET colleges. (4)

Discussion questions

1. Discuss communication as an instrumental function. (12)
2. When making decisions, government usually follows particular steps. Explain the decision-making process. (10)
3. Describe four things that must be considered with regards to furniture in the workplace. (8)
4. Explain the advantages of wearing uniforms and protective clothing in the workplace. (12)
5. Why is communication in the workplace important? (8)
6. Instrumental requirements can be personal or non-personal in nature. List five non-personal instrumental functions and briefly explain how they help to improve efficiency and effectiveness in the workplace. (20)

Grand total: 150

MODULE 6

FUNCTIONAL ACTIVITIES: LINE FUNCTIONS

This module covers the following aspects of line functions:

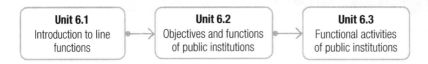

Unit 6.1	Unit 6.2	Unit 6.3
Introduction to line functions	Objectives and functions of public institutions	Functional activities of public institutions

Learning objectives

After completing this module, you should be able to do the following:

- Explain the nature and background of line functions
- Explain the objectives and functions of public institutions
- Describe each of the functional activities of public institutions.

Key terms

functional activities   line functions   objectives

Starting point

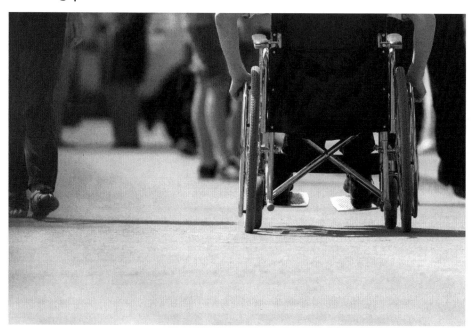

Figure 6.1 People with disabilities can benefit from social grants.

Noktula lives in Johannesburg and cares deeply about people with disabilities. One Saturday morning Noktula decided to visit the St Giles home for people with disabilities to see if she could help the residents. She discovered that there were 47 residents at St Giles who were benefitting from disability grants. The beneficiaries had different types of disabilities and were affected to varying degrees.

She learned that most of the beneficiaries did not have families nearby to support them. Some families of the residents were paying for their care while the rest relied on a disability grant to pay for their boarding. Noktula also learned that the Department of Social Development paid the disability grants to the beneficiaries and also paid the caregivers.

Without the disability grants, the beneficiaries would be unable to care for themselves both physically and emotionally. Noktula was very happy that the government was carrying out one of its functional activities of helping people with disabilities in the country.

In this module, you will learn more about the functional activities of government.

UNIT 6.1 Introduction to line functions

Every government has specific goals to achieve. You have learned that the main goal of any democratic government is to provide services to the public. In order to provide these services, government has to carry out a number of functions. Government functions are classified as:

- **Line functions:** they include order and protection, social welfare and economic welfare
- **Staff functions:** they include personnel services, resource supply services, accounting and auditing services, legal advisory services, financial services and office and secretarial services.

The objectives of government are achieved through the programmes and activities that take place in public institutions and government departments. Each government department or institution is identified by its functional activities, or **line functions**, which are the kind of services it provides to the public.

Basically, there are two main factors that determine the kind of functional activities that government institutions can undertake:

- The needs of the country: this includes basic needs such as food, nutrition, health services, education, water, sanitation, security and shelter
- The policy of the government of the day: this is determined by the ideology of the government.

We have learned that each government department is identified by the activities it provides or its line functions.

Line functions can be explained as the main purpose of an organisation, institution or department and the activities that define it. For example, the main purpose of the Department of Higher Education and Training is to provide higher education to the citizens of South Africa.

> **Did you know?** The goals of government are mainly achieved through the line functions of government, which take place in the various government departments and institutions.

Power break 6.1   GROUP WORK

1 In your groups, make a list of the needs of students at your college.
2 Discuss how you think the needs you have listed can be met and by whom.

> **DEFINITION**
>
> **line functions** – the main purpose of an organisation, institution or department and the activities that define it

Did you know? The Department of Social Development falls under the line functions of government. It is responsible for providing a number of social services to the public. Some of the services that are provided by the Department of Social Development include the following:

- National food relief
- Child protection services
- Adoption services
- Child support grants
- Disability grants
- Old age grants

Figure 6.2 The Minister of Social Development, Susan Shabangu, and the SASSA logo.

UNIT 6.2 Objectives and functions of public institutions

Throughout this course, you have learned that government provides services to the public through its own institutions and departments. This means government policy is executed through government departments and institutions through which:
- To provide services to the public
- To execute government policy
- To maintain law and order.

DEFINITION

objectives – things that need to be achieved

Figure 6.3 The University of Cape Town provides higher education services to the public.

The functions of public institutions are determined by the purpose for which they are established. This purpose originates from the ideology of the government of the day. Some governments believe in an ideology that promotes private enterprise or capitalism. Capitalism is an ideology that allows private ownership of the means of production, promotes competition and operates to make profit. Other governments would prefer socialism, an ideology that believes that all the means of production should be owned by the state. However, today, most countries have a mixed economy where they allow both public and private enterprises to operate simultaneously.

The number of **functional activities** that are carried out by public institutions are determined by the following:
- Ideology of the government of the day
- Demand from interest and pressure groups
- Physical characteristics of the state
- Social conditions prevailing in the country
- International political developments

Did you know? Communities are not able to satisfy their needs on their own; public institutions are established to satisfy these needs so that people in communities enjoy high-quality lives.

Key point: The most important services in South Africa are education, health and security.

DEFINITION

functional activities – activities that are essential to support the physical, social and psychological well-being of a person

Power break 6.2 INDIVIDUAL WORK

Read the following passage and answer the questions below.

The National Development Plan unpacked

The National Development Plan (NDP) offers a long-term perspective regarding the provision of social services in the country. It identifies a desired destination for South Africa and defines the role different sectors of society need to play in reaching that goal.

As a long-term strategic plan, it serves four broad objectives:

1 To provide overarching goals for what we want to achieve by 2030.
2 To build consensus on the key obstacles that might hinder the government from achieving these goals and what needs to be done to overcome the obstacles.
3 To provide a shared long-term strategic framework within which more detailed planning can take place in order to advance the long-term goals set out in the NDP.
4 To create a basis for making choices about how best to use limited resources.

The NDP aims to ensure that all South Africans attain a decent standard of living through the elimination of poverty and reduction of inequality. The core elements of a decent standard of living identified in the plan are:

- Housing, water, electricity and sanitation
- Safe and reliable public transport
- Quality education and skills development
- Safety and security
- Quality health care
- Social protection
- Employment
- Recreation and leisure
- Clean environment
- Adequate nutrition

Questions

1 What is meant by the letters NDP?
2 What are the main objectives of the NDP?
3 Explain what you understand by a decent standard of living and how it can be achieved.
4 Explain how poverty and inequality can be reduced in South Africa.
5 The NDP has identified core elements of a decent standard of living. Make a list of these core elements and for each suggest a government department or institution that you think is most suitable to provide the service.

Different public institutions and government departments provide specific services to the public. This is necessary because one public institution or department is not able to provide all the services that are demanded by the public. In this unit we discuss the functional activities of some of the public institutions and government departments in South Africa. The functional activities that will be discussed in this unit are classified as follows: education services; health services; law and order; protection services; regulation of labour affairs; agriculture, forestry and water affairs; public works and land affairs and transport.

Education services

Education refers to the systematic process of gaining knowledge and skills through study and instructions. Government has an obligation to provide education services to its people. The budget for education is usually the largest in South Africa. This is because government wants all the citizens of the country to improve their level of literacy and numeracy. The Constitution of the Republic of South Africa, Act 108 of 1996, provides that education is the right of every South African. This means that no one in the country must be denied the right to education.

Figure 6.4 Teachers and lecturers are employed by the government.

There are various reasons why education is very important in South Africa.

Figure 6.5 Education equips young people with skills and transforms the legacy of apartheid.

- It helps to transform the legacy of apartheid
- It helps to equip citizens with the much-needed skills to enable them to compete successfully in the work environment
- It helps to reduce the problem of poverty in the country
- It helps citizens to increase their chances of getting employed and to provide for their families.

In 2009, the government of South Africa made changes to the education portfolio in the country by creating two departments.

- **The Department of Basic Education:** this includes all schools from Grade R to Grade 12. It also includes adult literacy programmes such as Adult Basic Education (ABET).
- **Higher Education and Training:** this includes colleges and universities.

In order to promote education in the country, the government undertakes to do the following:

- Build educational institutions such as schools, colleges and universities
- Provide hostels and sports facilities for students
- Provide other requirements such as furniture, books and computers
- Provide educators; teachers and lecturers.

Case study

#FeesMustFall

Figure 6.6 Students protested against the increase in tertiary education fees as part of the #FeesMustFall movement.

According to the South African Constitution, 1996, all South Africans have the right to a basic education and no child can be excluded from school on grounds of race, religion or gender.

The demand for free education in South Africa started in 2015 when students started a protest movement code-named "FeesMustFall". This movement started at the University of Witwatersrand (Wits) in Johannesburg. It later spread to all the other universities in the country.

The demand for free education in South Africa is inherited from the Freedom Charter which, among other provisions, says the following about education in a new South Africa:

- Education shall be free, compulsory, universal and equal for all children;
- Higher education and technical training shall be opened to all by means of state allowances and scholarships awarded on the basis of merit;
- Adult illiteracy shall be ended by a mass state education plan;
- Teachers shall have all the rights of other citizens;
- The colour bar in cultural life, in sport and in education shall be abolished.

Questions

1 When did the demand for free education start in South Africa?
2 At which university did the protests for free education start?
3 What do you consider to be the main reason for the demand for free education in South Africa?
4 Do you think free education for all students in South Africa's tertiary institutions is possible? Give reasons for your answer.

Health services

The Department of Health is responsible for all health institutions and facilities in the country. There are health institutions such as hospitals, clinics and pharmacies through which health services are provided at all three levels of government.

Government satisfies the medical requirements for all public health institutions in the country. These requirements include medical facilities such as hospitals and clinics, medicines, ambulances, helicopters and the necessary personnel.

The South African Constitution of 1996 says that everyone has a right to access health care facilities in the country. It is the responsibility of the Department of Health to educate the public on all health matters and to ensure a healthy environment for all. The Department of Health provides many health services, which include the following:

- Street cleaning and refuse removal
- Controlling the spread of diseases such as cholera, HIV/AIDS and typhoid
- Preventing and combating infectious diseases by carrying out vaccination programmes
- Controlling the flow of medicines
- Building health institutions such as hospitals, clinics and health centres
- Satisfying medical requirements such as medicines, ambulances, helicopters and personnel.

Apart from the Constitution, the National Health Act, 61 of 2003, provides a framework for a structured and quality uniform health system in South Africa. It outlines the laws that govern national, provincial and local government with regard to health services. According to the National Health Act, no person may be refused emergency medical treatment and everyone has the right to an environment that is not harmful to their health.

Case study

Attacks on emergency personnel are a cause for concern

There is a growing concern over the increasing number of attacks on Emergency Medical Services (EMS) personnel in South Africa. Since 2012 more than 200 attacks on EMS personnel have been reported. In Nyanga township in Cape Town, four attacks on EMS personnel were reported in one day. Paramedics have also been attacked whilst on duty. Attacks on EMS personnel hinders the delivery of emergency healthcare to patients. It also has a direct impact on the ability of EMS personnel to provide efficient and effective services.

Figure 6.7 Ambulances and EMS personnel are vulnerable to attacks.

Questions

1 What do the letters EMS stand for?
2 How many attacks on EMS personnel have been reported since 2012?
3 In which township were four EMS attacks reported in one day?
4 Why do you think attacks on EMS personnel in South Africa is a cause for concern?

Law and order

The maintenance of law and order in South Africa is the responsibility of the Department of Police. According to the Constitution of 1996, the South African Police Service (SAPS) is responsible for the following:

- To prevent, combat and investigate crime
- Maintain public order
- To protect and secure the public and their property
- Uphold and enforce the law
- Create a safe and secure environment for all people in the country
- Investigate and prevent any crimes that threaten the safety or security of communities
- Ensure that criminals are brought to justice.

Municipal police help to maintain law and order in some municipalities. Municipal police are responsible for:

- Traffic policing
- Enforcing local by-laws within the local municipality
- Working with the SAPS to prevent crime
- Maintaining public order.

Figure 6.8 SAPS personnel work towards maintaining law and order in South Africa.

Did you know? Driving under the influence of alcohol and driving without a licence are both criminal offences in South Africa.

Protection services

Every country needs to defend itself against possible attacks from other nations. It is important that the government is always ready to defend and protect its citizens should there be a threat of an attack. The Department of Defence is responsible for defending the country and protecting its people through the South Africa National Defence Force (SANDF). Defending the country is a constitutional mandate. Chapter 11 of the South African Constitution, 1996 stipulates that:

* The SANDF should be structured and managed as a disciplined military force
* The primary function of the SANDF is to defend and protect the Republic of South Africa, its territorial integrity and its people.

The SANDF consists of a number of specialised units as follows:

* The army
* The navy
* The air force

Other protection services That are provided by other institutions in South Africa include the following:

* Firefighting
* Environmental conservation
* Prevention of water, air and land pollution

Figure 6.9 Environmental conservation falls under protection services.

Did you know? Firefighting is one of the protection services that is provided by government in South Africa. Firefighters help to protect people and their property, farms and the environment from destruction caused by fire.

Regulation of labour affairs

The South African government regulates labour affairs through the Department of Labour. The Department of Labour is responsible for all matters relating to employment. This includes matters relating to industrial relations, job creation, unemployment insurance and occupational health and safety. The department also protects the interests of both employers and employees. Employees must be protected against unfair labour practices, unemployment and injury on duty.

The following legislative guidelines help the Department of Labour to regulate labour affairs and the relationship between employers and employees.

Legislative guideline	Explanation
Labour Relations Act, 66 of 1995	• It applies to both employers and employees • It aims to advance economic development, social justice, harmonious labour relations and democracy at the workplace
Basic Conditions of Employment Act, 75 of 1997	• It applies to all employers and employees • It regulates working hours, employment contracts, deductions, payslips and termination of employment
Compensation for Occupational Injuries and Diseases Act	• Employees who are injured at work and those who get sick due to poor working conditions must be compensated
Employment Equity Act	• It applies to both employers and employees • It protects employees and job seekers from unfair discrimination • It provides a framework for implementing affirmative action
Occupational Health and Safety Act	• It provides and regulates health and safety at the workplace for all employees
Skills Development Act	• It aims to develop and improve the skills of all the workforce in the country
Unemployment Insurance Act, 63 of 2001	• It provides security to employees when they are unemployed • All employees must contribute to the Unemployment Insurance Fund (UIF) when they are still in employment

Agriculture, forestry and water affairs

Agriculture is an important economic activity in South Africa. It is sometimes referred to as the "backbone" of South Africa. This is because most of the raw materials that are used in various industries across the country are agricultural products. The Department of Agriculture, Forestry and Fisheries (DAFF) is responsible for all activities relating to agriculture, forestry and fishery in the country.

Much of the farmland in South Africa is owned by private enterprises and individuals. However, the DAFF is responsible for ensuring that the country has enough food to feed its people. In order to ensure food security and to promote agricultural activities in the country the department provides a number of functional activities, which include the following:
• Carrying out extensive research in various aspects of agriculture
• Providing education in the agricultural sector

- Controlling the standard and quality of agricultural products
- Regulating the marketing of agricultural products
- Undertaking pest control measures to prevent loss
- Conducting agricultural, veterinary and horticultural services
- Exercising control over agricultural remedies.

Figure 6.10 Agriculture is economically very important to South Africa.

The DAFF is also responsible for ensuring that the forest industry in the country is sustainable. The Forests Act, 84 of 1998 and the Forestry Laws Amendment Act, 35 of 2005 emphasise sustainable forest management. The Acts also explain how people and communities can use forests without destroying them. The Acts set out rules for protecting indigenous forests and ensuring that the public has reasonable access to state forests for the following purposes:
- Recreational purposes
- Cultural and spiritual purposes
- Educational purposes.

Functional activities of the Department of Agriculture, Forestry and Fisheries with regard to forestry include the following:
- Research and training to ensure sustainable management of forest resources
- Education and awareness programmes on the importance of forests
- Human resources development through commercial forestry activities such as forestation and downstream activities
- Encouraging co-operatives and job-creation activities such as afforestation.

Water is a critical commodity in the world. Water helps in sustainable socio-economic development and the eradication of poverty among communities. It is essential in our homes and is used for irrigation in the agricultural sector. The Department of Water and Sanitation (DWS) is responsible for administering water affairs in South Africa.

Figure 6.11 Waterworks in South Africa.

The DWS carries out various functional activities regarding water affairs in South Africa. These functional activities include the following:
- Raising awareness about the need to protect and conserve the country's water resources through education, training and awareness programmes
- Protecting and managing water sources
- Promoting equitable access to water
- Ensuring the delivery of effective water supply and sanitation
- Encouraging economic and efficient use of water
- Promoting research about water usage and water conservation.

Figure 6.12 Communal taps and water collection points will become increasingly common if rainfall does not improve.

The National Water Act, 36 of 1998 aims to ensure that water resources are protected, used, developed, conserved, managed and controlled in a sustainable manner for the benefit of the public.

> **Did you know?** In 2017, South Africa experienced its worst drought in recent memory. This has added to the serious water shortage in the country. The city of Cape Town was severely affected by the drought.

Public works and land affairs

The Department of Public Works (DPW) is responsible for all public works in the country. The responsibilities include the following:
- Providing accommodation and property management services to all the other government departments in the country
- Construction of buildings
- Purchase and sale of land
- Promoting the National Expanded Public Works Programme (NEPWP)
- Encouraging the transformation of the construction and property industries in the country.

The Department of Land Affairs is responsible for land rights to all citizens of South Africa. One of the main aims of this department is to assist previously disadvantaged individuals regarding land redistribution. The department aims to ensure productive land use and to have a well-planned human settlement programme.

Figure 6.13 RDP Houses in Soweto, South Africa, constructed by the Department of Public Works.

> **Did you know?** In order to have a well-planned human settlement programme, phase three of the District Six Redevelopment Project in Cape Town is underway. The project is aimed at returning all District Six claimants to the area as soon as possible and it aims to build 280 housing units.

Transport

Figure 6.14 Trains are an important aspect of public transport.

Efficient and reliable transport helps to improve economic and social development in a country. Imagine if there were no taxis, buses, trains or aeroplanes in South Africa. The government of South Africa is responsible for providing all forms of public transport in the country through the Department of Transport. The four main forms of transport in South Africa are: road, rail, air and sea.

Public transport in South Africa is regulated by the Department of Transport under the National Public Transport Regulator, which was established in terms of Section 20 of the National Transport Act, 5 of 2009. The main functions of the National Transport Regulator are to:

- Monitor and oversee public transport in the country
- Receive and decide on applications relating to inter-provincial operating licences, accreditation of tourist transport services and any other service designated by the Minister of Transport
- Oversee fares charged for public transport services throughout the country and advise the minister on the making of regulations in relation to fares or fare structures.

Did you know?

- The Department of Transport is responsible for transporting people and goods both inside and outside the country.
- Transport services in South Africa help to improve economic and social development.

Power break 6.3 GROUP WORK

Discuss functional activities with regard to the following:

1 Education services
2 Health services

WHAT DO WE KNOW AND WHERE TO NEXT...

Revisiting the learning objectives

Now that you have worked your way through this module, let's see if you have achieved the learning objectives that were set out at the beginning. In the table that follows we summarise the main concepts that you should know for each learning objective.

Learning objective	What you have learned
Explain the nature and background of line functions	• The aim of government is to provide services to the public. • Government services are provided through government departments. • Each government department or institution is identified by its functional activities or line functions; that is the kind of activities that it undertakes to provide services to the public. There are two factors that determine the functional activities that are under taken by government institutions or departments: • The needs of the country: this includes basic needs such as food, nutrition, health services, education, water, sanitation, security and shelter. • The policy of the government of the day: this is determined by the ideology of the government. A line function can be explained as follows: • The main purpose of an organisation and the activities that defines it.
Explain the objectives and functions of public institutions	• Basically, public institutions exist to provide services to the public and to execute government policy. Three main objectives of public institutions are: • To provide services to the public • To execute government policy • To maintain law and order. Public institutions include the following: public hospitals, correctional service facilities, welfare homes, clinics, public schools, colleges and universities. Different public institutions perform different functions. The number of functional activities that are carried out by public institutions are determined by the following: • Ideology of the government of the day • Demand from interest and pressure groups • Physical characteristics of the state • Social conditions prevailing in the country • International political developments.

Learning objective	What you have learned
Describe each of the functional activities of public institutions	Different public institutions perform different functional activities as follows: Education services: • Building educational institutions such as schools, colleges and universities • Providing hostels and sports facilities for students • Providing other requirements such as furniture, books and computers • Providing educators: teachers and lecturers. Health services: • Street cleaning and refuse removal • Controlling the spread of diseases such as cholera, HIV/AIDS and typhoid • Preventing and combating infectious diseases by carrying out vaccination programmes • Controlling the flow of medicines • Building health institutions such as hospitals, clinics and health centres • Providing medical requirements such as medicines, ambulances, helicopters and personnel. Law and order: By the SAPS: • Prevent, combat and investigate crime • Maintain public order • Protect, secure the public and their property • Uphold and enforce the law • Create a safe and secure environment for all people in the country • Investigate and prevent any crimes that threaten the safety or security of communities • Ensure that criminals are brought to justice. By municipal police: • Traffic policing • Enforcing municipal by-laws • Working with the SAPS to prevent crime • Maintaining public order. Protection services: • The SANDF protects the country and its people against foreign attacks. Other protection services that are provided by other institutions in South Africa include the following: • Firefighting • Environmental conservation • Prevention of water, air and land pollution Regulation of labour affairs: The Department of Labour regulates matters relating to: • Industrial relations • Job creation • Unemployment insurance • Occupational health and safety. The department also protects the interests of both employers and employees. Employees must be protected against: • Unfair labour practices • Unemployment • Injury on duty.

Learning objective	What you have learned
	Agriculture, forestry and water affairs:

Agriculture:

- Carrying out extensive research in various aspects of agriculture
- Providing education in the agricultural sector
- Controlling the standard and quality of agricultural products
- Regulating the marketing of agricultural products
- Undertaking pest control measures to prevent loss
- Conducting agricultural, veterinary and horticultural services
- Exercising control over agricultural remedies.

Forestry:

- Research and training to ensure sustainable management of forest resources
- Education and awareness programmes on the importance of forests
- Human resources development through commercial forestry activities such as forestation and downstream activities
- Encouraging co-operatives and job creation activities such as tree planting projects or afforestation.

Water affairs:

- Raising awareness about the need to protect and conserve the country's water resources through education, training and awareness programmes
- Protecting and managing water sources
- Promoting equitable access to water
- Ensuring the delivery of effective water supply and sanitation
- Encouraging economic and efficient use of water
- Promoting research about water usage and water conservation

Public Works and Land Affairs:

Public Works:

- Providing accommodation and property management services to all the other government departments in the country
- Construction of buildings
- Purchase and sale of land
- Promoting the National Expanded Public Works Programme (NEPWP)
- Encouraging the transformation of the construction and property industries in the country.

Land Affairs:

- Ensuring land rights for all South Africans
- Emphasising previously disadvantaged individuals regarding land redistribution
- Ensuring productive use of land
- Developing a well-planned human settlement programme for the country.

Transport:

- Monitor and oversee public transport in the country
- Receive and decide on applications relating to inter-provincial operating licences, accreditation of tourist transport services and any other service designated by the Minister of Transport
- Oversee fares charged for public transport services throughout the country and advise the Minister on the making of regulations in relation to fares or fare structures. |

True or false

Indicate whether the following statements are TRUE or FALSE. Write only "true" or "false" and the correct question number.

1. Public institutions are identified by their line functions.
2. Public transport in South Africa is controlled by the taxi industry.
3. All public institutions perform the same government functions.
4. Afforestation is the cutting down of trees in a large area.
5. Employment equity applies to both the employer and the employee. (5 × 2) [10]

Abbreviations

What do these abbreviations stand for?

1.	ABET	6.	UIF
2.	SASSA	7.	DAFF
3.	NDP	8.	DWS
4.	SAPS	9.	DPW
5.	SANDF	10.	NEPWP

(10 × 2) [20]

Definitions

Define the following terms:

1. Capitalism
2. Education
3. Socialism
4. Line function
5. Afforestation (5 × 2) [10]

Match the columns

Match the term in Column A to the correct description in Column B.

Column A		Column B	
1.	Forestry	A.	The main purpose of an organisation and the activities that define it
2.	SANDF	B.	Maintains law and order
3.	Line functions	C.	Receives and decides on applications relating to inter-provincial operating licences, accreditation of tourist transport services
4.	Land affairs	D.	Protects the country against foreign attacks
5.	Transport	E.	Encouraging co-operatives and job creation activities such as tree planting projects or afforestation
		F.	Emphasises previously disadvantaged individuals regarding land redistribution

(5 × 2) [10]

Short questions

1. Name two factors that determine the functional activities that are performed by institutions. (4)
2. Name three line functions that are undertaken by government. (6)
3. Explain what you understand by the term line function. (2)
4. List the functional activities of municipal police. (8)
5. The SANDF consists of a number of specialised units. Name these units. (6)
6. In 2009, the government of South Africa made changes to the education portfolio in the country by creating two departments. Name the two departments that are concerned with education in South Africa. (4)

Long questions

1. Discuss the three main objectives of public institutions. (6)
2. Discuss functional activities of public institutions with regard to the following:
   a) Transport (6)
   b) Agriculture, forestry and water affairs (18)
   c) Public works and land affairs (18)
   d) Law and order (20)
3. Explain the main functions of the National Transport Regulator. (6)
4. The Forests Act, 84 of 1998 and the Forestry Laws Amendment Act, 35 of 2005 set out rules for protecting indigenous forests. What is the purpose of protecting indigenous forests? (6)

Grand total: 160

GOVERNMENTAL RELATIONSHIPS

This module covers the following aspects of governmental relationships:

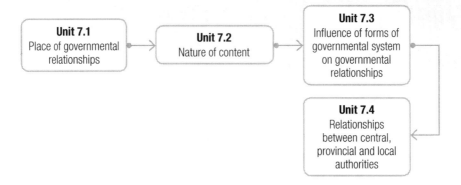

Unit 7.1
Place of governmental relationships

Unit 7.2
Nature of content

Unit 7.3
Influence of forms of governmental system on governmental relationships

Unit 7.4
Relationships between central, provincial and local authorities

Learning objectives

After completing this module, you should be able to do the following:

- Explain the place of governmental relationships
- Describe the nature of the content
- Explain the influence of forms of government on governmental relationships
- Explain the relationships between central, provincial and local authorities

Key terms

central government	intergovernmental	local government
content	relationships	provincial government

Starting point

Figure 7.1 Shireen has just learned about the structure of government in South Africa.

Shireen has just attended a lecture on the structure of government. She has learned that the structure of government in South Africa consists of three spheres and three arms.

The three spheres of government make up a hierarchy with the central government on the top in the highest position, followed by the provincial level and then the local level. She also learned that the three arms of government include the legislature, the executive and the judiciary, which are not hierarchical, but horizontal in nature.

Shireen has also just learned how relationships in both the three spheres of government and the three arms of government take place.

In this module, you will learn more about governmental relationships.

UNIT 7.1 Place of governmental relationships

The Constitution of the Republic of South Africa, 1996, provides for both the three spheres of government and the three arms of government in the country. Section 41 of the Constitution, 1996, establishes the need and importance for co-operation and interaction between the three spheres of government and between the three arms of government.

The interaction and co-operation that takes place within the three spheres of government is called **intergovernmental relations**. This is the mutual relationship that exists among government institutions or government structures. The Constitution further establishes that the country must be run on a system of co-operative governance. This means there must be co-operation between the three spheres of government. This co-operation and interaction is referred to as governmental relationship.

The three levels of government include the **central government**, **provincial government** and the **local government**. There is a need for the interaction and co-operation between the three levels of government so that they are effective and efficient in providing services to the public. Co-operation and interaction between the three levels of government also help to ensure uniformity and consistency in the delivery of services and to ensure effective control.

Throughout this course you have learned that there are three arms of government, which are the legislature, the judiciary and the executive. The three arms of government have been decentralised to all the three spheres of government as follows:

Government level/Sphere	Legislature	Executive	Administration
Central/National	Parliament	President and Cabinet	Director General and departments
Provincial	Provincial legislature	Premier and Member of the Executive Council (MECs)	Heads of departments and staff
Local	Municipal council	Mayor and the Mayoral Committee	Municipal Manager, heads of departments and staff

Did you know? Governmental relations in South Africa is a constitutional matter.

DEFINITIONS

intergovernmental relationships – the mutual relations that exist among government institutions or government structures

central government – the highest level of government, the national government

provincial government – also known as provincial authority; government at the level of provinces

local government – the lowest level of government; has authority on a municipal level

The structure of government in South Africa is seen through the interaction that takes place between the three spheres of government on one hand and the three arms of government on the other hand. The three spheres of government in South Africa follow a hierarchical structure as follows:

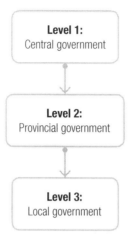

Level 1:
Central government

Level 2:
Provincial government

Level 3:
Local government

Unlike the three spheres of government, which are hierarchical, the three arms of government in South Africa are horizontal. They include the legislature, the judiciary and the executive, and they are structured as follows:

The legislature → The executive → The judiciary

Figure 7.2 National legislation that regulates the daily operations of municipalities is debated and agreed on by government in Parliament.

UNIT 7.2 Nature of content

Governmental relationships can be viewed as the mutual relationships that exists between the three spheres of government. This includes the relationship regarding the powers and functions of each sphere of government and the nature of supervision that takes place at each sphere of government.

Governmental relationships can be divided into three categories, as follows:

- Intergovernmental relations
- Intragovernmental relations
- Extra-governmental relations.

Intergovernmental relations refer to the mutual relations that exist among government institutions or government structures. Intergovernmental relations can be vertical or horizontal.

Figure 7.3 Municipalities belong to the local level of government.

Vertical intergovernmental relations:

- This refers to the relationship between governmental bodies in different spheres of government, such as the relationship between governmental bodies at central, provincial and local government levels.
- The higher authority (central government) has more power than the subordinate authorities (provincial or local government).
- Lower authorities largely depend on the higher authorities when they require some facilities that will enable them to achieve their objectives.
- The dependency of subordinate authorities on higher authorities restricts the amount of discretion enjoyed by subordinate bodies in deciding which community values should be implemented (dependence on such facilities as finance and policy).
- However, there is also some degree of interdependence between the governmental bodies at lower levels.

> **DEFINITION**
>
> **content** – refers to everything that forms part of governmental relations

- The nature of government structure and the ideology of government will determine the nature of vertical intergovernmental relations.

Figure 7.4 The three spheres of government must work together.

Horizontal intergovernmental relations:
- This refers to the relationships between governmental bodies that are in the same tier or level of government. The relationship between the nine provincial authorities in South Africa is an example of horizontal intergovernmental relations.
- Interaction and co-operation between governmental bodies is mainly centred on discussions regarding physical and information assistance and not necessarily on policy and finance as in vertical intergovernmental relations. For example, assistance at local government level may involve traffic services, sewers and the fire brigade.

Intragovernmental relations refer to the relations taking place within any of the three spheres of government. For example, the relationship between the finance department and the personnel department or procurement department of a particular municipality.

Extra-governmental relations refer to the relations between a government structure and a non-government actor such as the community.

Governmental divisions exacerbate water crisis in Cape Town

According to David Olivier, a postdoctoral research fellow at the Global Change Institute of the University of the Witwatersrand, two spheres of governance – the Western Cape province and the City of Cape Town – prepared adequately for drought. The system failed, however, at the level of national government.

Since at least December 2015 the Western Cape provincial government and the City of Cape Town have appeared to lay the blame for the water crisis on the national Water and Sanitation Department and its minister, Nomvula Mokonyane.

Since 2015 the Western Cape has been experiencing a drought which has depleted the province's dams and thrown the City of Cape Town into extreme water shortages. In 2015, the Western Cape government appealed to national government for R35 million to increase water supplies by drilling boreholes and recycling water. National government rejected the request at that stage, possibly because dams were still 75% full.

The following year, national government agreed to recognise five of the 30 Western Cape municipalities as drought disaster areas. Noticeably, Cape Town was not included. Then, by October 2017, national government had still not released the promised funds. The Cape Town Mayor appealed directly to the Department of Water and Sanitation for disaster relief funding. But this was rejected on the grounds that Cape Town was "not yet at crisis level".

South African Water Caucus, a civil society group, has revealed that national government's reluctance to provide drought relief funding stemmed from increasing debt, corruption and mismanagement in the national Department of Water and Sanitation. However, DA leader Mmusi Maimane said "now is not the time for politicking and finger-pointing. We do not have the luxury of time. We need to unite behind this common mission to defeat Day Zero".

Figure 7.5 Cape Town's drought has been exacerbated by the three spheres of government failing to work together efficiently.

continued on the next page …

UNIT 7.3 Influence of forms of governmental system on governmental relationships

The form of governmental system in any country has great influence on governmental relationships. In this unit we discuss the influence of two forms of government on governmental relations: the unitary form of government and the federal form of government.

The unitary form of government

A unitary form of government can be defined as a sovereign state where the central government has supreme authority to govern. This means all the authority of government is centralised at national government level. The administrative divisions of government only exercise powers that have been delegated to them by the central government. Final decisions in any matter affecting the country are made by central government.

A unitary state is characterised by the following principles:

- All power is placed in one central governing system
- The different regions within the country may at most times lack the authority to establish their own laws, especially in purely unitary systems
- Resources are shared from the central government to the different regions within the country
- All major government decisions are made by the central government
- The national legislative authority is empowered to promulgate, approve and amend laws
- The legislative authority may create financial resources and establish executive institutions for the rendering of its functions
- The legislative authority may assign powers, authority and financial resources to spheres of government and determine and regulate governmental relations
- Many unitary governments end up either as dictators or totalitarians. Examples include the Great Britain and the Ukraine.

The federal form of government

The federal form of government can be defined as a form of government where there is division of power between two levels of government: central government and provincial government. At central government level, all matters of common interest to the entire country are addressed while those that affect only the provincial government are addressed by the respective province.

A federal form of government is characterised by the following:
- Power is distributed from central government to provincial government. The lower government authorities can exercise control within their area of jurisdiction without interference from central government
- Laws established by local government institutions should be in line with the fundamental laws of central government. An example of a federal government can be found in the United States of America.

Figure 7.6 The White House is where the President of the United States of America lives and works.

Key points:

- Governmental relationships in a unitary system of government differ significantly from those in a federal system of government.
- In a unitary system all power is centralised at central government level and in a federal system power is distributed from central government to lower government levels.

Power break 7.1   GROUP WORK

In your groups, discuss what you think are the advantages and disadvantages of:

1 The unitary form of government
2 The federal form of government

UNIT 7.4 Relationships between central, provincial and local authorities

STOP VIOLENCE AGAINST WOMEN

Figure 7.7 The spheres of government co-operate to promote campaigns, such as the 16 days of no violence against women and children.

Intergovernmental relations include continuous exchange of information and views where government policy is generated by interactions among public officials in different spheres of government. The South African Constitution, 1996, establishes a state that supports continuous interaction and co-operation between the three spheres of government. In this unit we discuss the nature of relationships that exist between the three spheres of government in South Africa.

Relations between central government and provincial government

The relationship between central government and provincial government is provided by the Constitution. This relationship is more supervisory in nature; where central government supervises the operations of provincial government. For example:

- Section 125(2) of the Constitution outlines the constitutional duty of the Provincial Executive to implement all national legislation and to co-ordinate the functions of the provincial administration and its departments
- Section 100(1)(b) of the Constitution gives national government the power to intervene when a province cannot or does not fulfil its executive obligation in terms of legislation.

Central government can only intervene in the operations of a province when the provincial authority fails to fulfil its executive obligation as required by the Constitution or any other legislation. Such intervention should state the steps that the province must take to meet its obligation or to assume responsibility for the relevant obligation in the province.

The intervention of central government in the operations of a province is necessary for the following reasons:
- To maintain essential national standards
- To meet minimum standards for the rendering of services
- To maintain economic unity
- To maintain national security
- To prevent some provinces from taking unreasonable actions that prejudice the interest of other provinces or the country.

The steps for the intervention requires that:
- The notice of intervention must be tabled in the National Council of Provinces within 14 days of its first sitting after the intervention began by a Cabinet member responsible for provincial affairs.
- The notice must be accompanied by a memorandum explaining the reasons for the intervention.
- The Chairperson of the Council should refer the matter to the select committee responsible for constitutional affairs.
- The intervention must end unless it is approved by Council within 30 days of its first sitting after intervention has begun.
- The Council must review the intervention regularly and must make appropriate recommendations to the national executive.

Relations between central government and local government

Local government is the lowest sphere of government authority in South Africa. Relations between central government and local government are governed by the Constitution and other forms of legislation. Relations between central government and local government are characterised by the following:
- Central government and local government must maintain a co-operative and constructive relationship rather than a competitive one.
- Local government is not totally autonomous because central government makes laws that affect local government, for example, laws that affect the entire country such as laws on housing, roads and labour.
- Local government must be part of the political and administrative system of the whole country, they must, therefore, implement decisions and policies made by central government.
- Legislative authority is vested in Parliament, which ultimately controls all government activities including activities of local government.

- Local government must have a system of communicating with central government where the two operate in common fields such as tourism, sport and health.

Figure 7.8 Street lights in Botshabelo, Free State province. Local government (Mangaung Metropolitan Municipality) and Free State province need to work together to ensure that residents have essential services such as lighting, which helps to keep communities safe.

Relations between local government and provincial government

The relationship between local government and provincial government is a constitutional matter. Section 155(6) of the Constitution requires provincial governments to promote the development and capacity of local government. In this regard, the nature of the relationship between local government and provincial government can be explained as follows:

- Provincial government must play a key role in monitoring, supporting and strengthening the capacity of local government to ensure the maintenance of good governance and high standard of public service and good governance.
- If a bill from central government or provincial government affects the status, institutions, powers or functions of local government, it must be published in the official gazette so that the public can have the opportunity to make representations.
- Local governments can make and administer by-laws that will enable them to effectively manage matters within their jurisdiction. However, such by-laws will be invalid if they are in conflict with central and provincial legislation.
- Central or provincial government may only delegate tasks to local government if the local government has the capacity to perform them.
- Delegation of matters from provincial government to local government should only be done if the matter can be administered more effectively at local government level and if the local government has the capacity to do so.
- Delegation of matters from provincial government must be a result of a decision by the provincial Executive Council and it should follow consultations with the local government concerned within the province.

- Local government may also be asked by the premier to follow a certain course of action or restrain them from pursuing policies that do not improve the welfare of the community.
- A local government has the right to exercise any power concerning a matter reasonably necessary for the effective performance of its function.

Figure 7.9 The Northwest High Court, Mahikeng.

In terms of Section 139 (1) (b) of the Constitution, 1996, provincial government can intervene in local government affairs when local government fails to perform its constitutional obligation. When provincial government intervenes in the affairs of local government, the following must be considered:

- The provincial government must issue a directive stating the steps that are required to meet the obligation of the local government or assuming responsibility for the relevant obligation in order to:
  - maintain standards
  - prevent the local government from taking an unreasonable action
  - maintain economic unity.
- The intervention must end within 14 days of the commencement of the intervention, unless its continuation is approved by the cabinet member responsible for local government affairs.
- If a directive from provincial government has not been complied with, the provincial Executive Council will assume responsibility for the relevant obligation in the local government.
- The provincial executive should submit a written notice of the intervention to the cabinet minister responsible for local government affairs to review the intervention within 14 days after the intervention has started.

> **Did you know?** The premier of a province may approve or disapprove proposals made by local government authorities depending on the impact such decisions have on the local community.

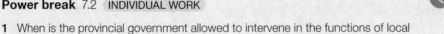

Power break 7.2   INDIVIDUAL WORK

1 When is the provincial government allowed to intervene in the functions of local government?
2 Why do you think the intervention of central government in the operations of a province is necessary?
3 Discuss what happens if a directive from a provincial government has not been complied with by a local government.

WHAT DO WE KNOW AND WHERE TO NEXT...

Revisiting the learning objectives

Now that you have worked your way through this module, let's see if you have achieved the learning objectives that were set out at the beginning. In the table that follows we summarise the main concepts that you should know for each learning objective.

Learning objective	What you have learned
Explain the place of governmental relationships	• The Constitution of the Republic of South Africa provides for both the three spheres of government and the three arms of government in the country. • Section 41 of the Constitution establishes the need and importance for co-operation and interaction between the three levels of government. • This interaction and co-operation that takes place within the various levels of government and the three arms of government is called intergovernmental relations. • The three levels of government include the central government, provincial government and the local government. • The Constitution further establishes that the country must be run on a system of co-operative governance. • This is because the main purpose of government is to provide services to its people. • Co-operation and interaction among the three levels of government helps to ensure uniformity and effectiveness in the delivery of services and to ensure effective control.
Describe the nature of the content	• Governmental relationships take place among the three spheres of government. • They include the relationship regarding the powers and functions of each sphere of government and the nature of supervision that takes place at each sphere of government. Governmental relationships can be divided into three categories as follows: • Intergovernmental relations • Intragovernmental relations • Extra-governmental relations. **Intergovernmental relations** refer to the mutual relations that exist within government structures and can be vertical or horizontal. Vertical intergovernmental relations: • This refers to the relationship between governmental bodies in different spheres of government such as the relationship between governmental bodies at central, provincial and local government levels. • The higher authority (central government) has more power than the subordinate authorities (provincial or local government).

Learning objective	What you have learned
	• Lower authorities largely depend on the higher authorities when they require some facilities that will enable them to achieve their objectives. • The dependency of subordinate authorities on higher authorities restricts them on the measure of discretion enjoyed by subordinate bodies in deciding which community values should be implemented (dependent on such facilities as finance and policy). Horizontal intergovernmental relations: • They refer to the relationships between governmental bodies that are at the same level of government. • Interaction and co-operation between governmental bodies is mainly centred on discussions regarding physical and information assistance and not necessarily on policy and finance as in vertical intergovernmental relations **Intragovernmental relations** refer to the relations taking place within any of the three spheres of government. **Extra-governmental relations** refer to the relations between a government structure and a non-government actor such as the community.
Explain the influence of forms of government on governmental relationships	The form of governmental system in any country has great influence on governmental relationships. **The unitary form of government** • A unitary form of government is where all the authority of government is centralised at national government level. • The administrative divisions of government only exercise powers that have been delegated to them by the central government. • Final decisions in any matter affecting the country are made by central government. Principles of a unitary form of government can be summarised as follows: • All power is placed in one central governing system • The different regions within the country may at most times lack the authority to establish their own laws especially in purely unitary systems • Resources are shared from the central government to the different regions within the country • All major government decisions are made by the central government • The national legislative authority is empowered to promulgate, approve and amend laws • The legislative authority may create financial resources and establish executive institutions for the rendering of its functions • The legislative authority may assign powers, authority and financial resources to spheres of government and determine and regulate governmental relations • Many unitary governments end up either as dictatorships or totalitarian states. **The federal form of government** • It is a form of government where power is divided between central government and provincial government.

Learning objective	What you have learned
	• At central government level, all matters of common interest to the entire country are addressed while those that affect only the provincial governments are addressed within the respective provinces.
	A federal form of government is characterised by the following:
	• Power is distributed from central government to provincial government
	• The lower government authorities can exercise control within their area of jurisdiction without interference from central government
	• Laws established by local government institutions should be in line with the fundamental laws of central government.
Explain the relationships between central, provincial and local authorities	Continuous interaction and co-operation between the three spheres of government is very important in order to improve efficiency and effectiveness.
	Relations between central government and provincial government
	The relationship between central government and provincial government is provided by the Constitution. Example:
	• Section 125 (2) of the Constitution outlines the constitutional duty of the Provincial Executive to implement all national legislation and to co-ordinate the functions of the provincial administration and its departments
	• Section 100 (1) (b) of the Constitution gives national government the power to intervene when a province cannot or does not fulfil its executive obligation in terms of legislation.
	The relationship between central government and provincial government is more supervisory in nature. Central government supervises the operations of provincial government.
	Central government can intervene in the operations of provincial government if the provincial government fails to fulfil its executive obligation as required by the Constitution or any other legislation. The intervention should state the steps that the province must take to meet its obligation or to assume responsibility for the relevant obligation in the province. The intervention of central government in the operations of provincial government is necessary for the following reasons:
	• To maintain essential national standards
	• To meet minimum standards for the rendering of services
	• To maintain economic unity
	• To maintain national security
	• To prevent some provinces from taking unreasonable actions that prejudice the interest of other provinces or the country.
	The steps for the intervention requires that:
	• The notice of intervention must be tabled in the National Council of Provinces within 14 days of its first sitting after the intervention began by a Cabinet member responsible for provincial affairs
	• The notice must be accompanied by a memorandum explaining the reasons for the intervention
	• The Chairperson of the Council should refer the matter to the select committee responsible for constitutional affairs

Learning objective	What you have learned
	• The intervention must end unless it is approved by Council within 30 days of its first sitting after intervention has began • The Council must review the intervention regularly and must make appropriate recommendations to the national executive. **Relations between central government and local government** Local government is the lowest sphere of government authority in South Africa. Relations between central government and local government are a constitutional matter and are characterised by the following: • Central government and local government must maintain a co-operative and constructive relationship rather than a competitive one • Local government is not totally autonomous because central government makes laws that affect local government • Local government must be part of the political and administrative system of the whole country. They must, therefore, implement decisions and policies made by central government • Legislative authority is vested in Parliament, which ultimately controls all government activities including activities of local government • Local government must have a system of communicating with central government where the two operate in common fields such as tourism, sport and health. **Relations between local government and provincial government** The relationship between local government and provincial government is a constitutional matter. Section 155(6) of the Constitution requires provincial governments to promote the development and capacity of local government. The nature of the relationship between local government and provincial government can be explained as follows: • Provincial government must play a key role in monitoring, supporting and strengthening the capacity of local government to ensure the maintenance of good governance and high standard of public service and good governance • If a bill from central government or provincial government affects the status, institutions, powers or functions of local government, it must be published in the official gazette so that the public can have the opportunity to make representations • Local governments can make and administer by-laws that will enable them to effectively manage matters within their jurisdiction. However, such by-laws will be invalid if they are in conflict with central and provincial legislation • Central or provincial government may only delegate tasks to local government if the local government has the capacity to perform them • Delegation of matters from provincial government to local government should only be done if the matter can be administered more effectively at local government level and if the local government has the capacity to do so

Learning objective	What you have learned
	• Delegation of matters from provincial government must be a result of a decision by the provincial Executive Council and it should follow consultations with the local government concerned within the province
	• Local government may also be asked by the premier to follow a certain course of action or restrain them from pursuing policies that do not improve the welfare of the community
	• A local government has the right to exercise any power concerning a matter reasonably necessary for the effective performance of its function.
	In terms of Section 139(1)(b) of the Constitution, 1996, provincial government can intervene in local government affairs when the local government fails to perform its constitutional obligation. When provincial government intervenes in the affairs of local government, the following must be considered:
	• The provincial government must issue a directive stating the steps that are required to meet the obligation of the local government or assuming responsibility for the relevant obligation in order to:
	– maintain standards
	– prevent the local government from taking an unreasonable action
	– maintain economic unity.
	• The intervention must end within 14 days of the commencement of the intervention, unless its continuation is approved by the Cabinet member responsible for local government affairs.
	• If a directive from provincial government has not been complied with, the provincial Executive Council will assume responsibility for the relevant obligation in the local government.
	• The provincial executive should submit a written notice of the intervention to the Cabinet minister responsible for local government affairs to review the intervention within 14 days after the intervention has started.

Assessment

True or false

Indicate whether the following statements are TRUE or FALSE. Write only "true" or "false" next to the correct question number.

1. Co-operative governance means co-operation among the three spheres of government.
2. Governmental relations in South Africa is a constitutional matter.
3. Local government must be part of the political and administrative system of the whole country.
4. Central government and local government must maintain a competitive relationship rather than a constructive relationship.
5. In a federal form of government, all power is placed in one central government.
6. The relation between central government and provincial government is an example of horizontal intergovernmental relations.
7. Local governments can make and administer by-laws that are in conflict with central and provincial legislation.
8. The intervention of central government in the operations of a province helps to maintain economic unity.
9. Intergovernmental relations is the relationship between a government structure and a non-government actor.
10. Notice of intervention must be accompanied by a memorandum explaining the reasons for the intervention. (10 x 2) [20]

Definitions

Define the following terms:

1. Governmental relationship
2. Intergovernmental relations
3. Intragovernmental relations
4. Unitary form of government
5. Federal form of government
6. Extra-governmental relations
7. Vertical intergovernmental relations
8. Horizontal intergovernmental relations (8 x 2) [16]

Match the columns

Match the term in Column A to the correct description in Column B.

Column A		Column B	
1.	Federal form of government	A.	Should submit a written notice of the intervention to the Cabinet minister responsible for local government affairs to review the intervention within 14 days after the intervention has started
2.	Reason for intervention by central government	B.	Power is concentrated at central government level
3.	Extra-governmental relations	C.	The mutual relations that exist within government structures and can be vertical or horizontal
4.	Provincial Executive	D.	Establishes that the country must be run on a system of co-operative governance
5.	Intergovernmental relations	E.	Laws established by local government
6.	Unitary form of government	F.	The relations between a government structure and a non-government actor such as the community
7.	Constitution	G.	The relations taking place within any of the three spheres of government
		H.	To meet minimum standards for rendering services

(7 x 2) [14]

Short questions

1. Name the two forms of intergovernmental relations. (4)
2. List five reasons why intervention by central government in the operations of a province is necessary. (10)
3. Name the three spheres of government in South Africa. (6)
4. Briefly explain the following:
    a) Intergovernmental relations
    b) Vertical intergovernmental relations
    c) Horizontal intergovernmental relations
    d) Intragovernmental relations
    e) Extra-governmental relations

    (10)

Long questions

1. The relationship between central government and provincial government is provided by the Constitution. Explain how the Constitution provides the relationship. (4)
2. Explain the principles of a unitary form of government. (16)
3. Discuss the characteristics of a federal form of government. (6)
4. Explain the difference between a unitary form of government and a federal form of government. (4)

5. Explain the steps that must be followed when central government intervenes in the function of a provincial government. (10)
6. Discuss the place of governmental relationships in South Africa. (14)
7. Discuss the nature of relationship between local government and provincial government. (16)

Grand total: 150

REFERENCES

Anderson, J.E. 1997. *Public policy making*. Boston: Houghton Mifflin.

Berning, J., De Beer, A., Du Toit, D., Kriel, G., Kriel, J., Louw, H., Mouton, J., Rossouw, D. and Singh, D. 2005. *Focus on management principles: a generic approach*. Lansdowne: Juta.

Black, H.M.S. and Porter, L.W. 2004. *Management*. Englewood Cliffs, NJ: Prentice Hall.

Borins, S.F. 1995. "The New Public Management is Here to Stay," Canadian Public Administration (Spring): 122–132.

Botes, P.S., Brynard, P.A., Fourie, D.J., Roux, N.L. 1992. *Public Administration and Management: A guide to central, regional and municipal administration and management*. Pretoria: Van Schaik.

Cloete, J.J.N. and Thornhil, C. 2005. *South African Municipal Government Administration: A new dispensation*. Johannesburg: Dotsquare Publishing.

Das, T.K. 1994. Educating tomorrow's managers: The role of critical thinking. *The international Journal of Organizational Analysis*, 2 (4), Oct.

Du Toit, D.F.P. and Van der Waldt, G. 1999. *Public Administration and management –The Grassroots*. 2nd ed. Kenwyn: Juta.

Dye, T.R. 1995. *Understanding public policy*. Englewood Cliffs, NJ: Prentice-Hall.

English Oxford Living Dictionaries https://en.oxforddictionaries.com/definition/procedure (Accessed 21 July 2017).

Flamholtz, E.G. 1996. *Effective management control: Theory and practice*. London: Kluwer Academic Publishers.

Fox, W. and Meyer, I.M. 1995. *Public Administration dictionary*. Cape Town: Juta.

Fox, W., Schwella, E. and Wissink, H. 1991. *Public Management*. Cape Town: Juta & Co. Ltd.

Government of Manitoba. About records. https://www.gov.mb.ca/chc/archives/gro/record-keeping/about_records.html (Access date: 22 October 2017).

Greene, J.D. 2005. *Public Administration in the new century: a concise introduction*. Belmont: Wadsworth.

Grusenmeyer, D. 2003. Developing effective standard operating procedures https://ecommons.cornell.edu/bitstream/handle/1813/36910/sopsdir.pdf;sequence=1 (Access date: 04 August 2017).

Hattingh, J.J. 1998. *Governmental relations: A South African perspective*. Pretoria: UNISA Press.

Hood, C. 1991. "A Public Management for all Seasons." *Public Administration* vol. 69/1 (Spring): 3–20.

Hughes, O.E. 2003. *Public Management and Administration: an introduction*. 3rd edition. New York: MacMillan.

Jones, L.R., and Thompson, F. 1999. *Public Management: Institutional Renewal for the 21st Century*. Stamford, CT: JAI-Elsevier Science.

Jones, R.G. 2004. *Organizational Theory, Design, and Change*. Upper Saddle River, NJ: Prentice Hall.

Judge, T.A. and Heneman, H.G. 2006. *Staffing Organizations*. Boston, MA: McGraw-Hill-Irwin.

Koelble, T. 2011. Too many obstacles to service delivery at local government level http://citizen.co.za/news/news-national/382924/14-740-service-delivery-protests-recorded-in-sa/ (Accessed: 20 July 2017).

Levy, N. and Tapscott, C. 2001. *Intergovernmental relations in South Africa: The challenges and co-operative government*. Bellville: IDASA and School of Government, University of the Western Cape.

Mukwindidza, E. *Succeed in Public Administration. N5 Student book*. Cape Town: Oxford University Press.

Parliament of the Republic of South Africa. https://www.parliament.gov.za/what-parliament-does (Accessed: 18 August 2017).

Republic of South Africa. 1996. *The Constitution of the Republic of South Africa, 1996*. Pretoria: Government Printer.

Robert, N.A. 1988. *The management control function*. 5th edition. Califonia: Harvard Business School Press.

Smith, P.J. and Cronje, P G.L. 1992. *Management principles: A contemporary South African edition*. Kenwyn: Juta & Co. Ltd.

South Africa. Basic Conditions of Employment Act, 75 of 1997.

South Africa. Constitution of the Republic of South Africa, 1996.

South Africa. Forestry Laws Amendment Act, 35 of 2005.

South Africa. Forests Act, 84 of 1998.

South Africa. Labour Relations Act, No. 66 of 1995.

South Africa. National Health Act, 61 of 2003.

South Africa. National Transport Act, 5 of 2009.

South Africa. National Water Act, 36 of 1998.

South Africa. Unemployment Insurance Act, 63 of 2001.

Thompson, F. 1997. "The New Public Management," *Journal of Policy Analysis and Management.* 16/1: 165–176.

Thornhill, C. and Hanekom, S.X. 1995. *The Public-Sector Manager*. Durban: Butterworths.

Thornhill, C., Ondendaal, M.J., Malan, L.P., Mathebula, F.M., Van Dijk, H.G. and Mello, D.M. 2002. *An overview of intergovernmental relations in South Africa: Southern African Development Community*. Pretoria: PAIR Institute.

Van der Waldt, G. and Du Toit, D.F.P. 1997. *Managing for excellence in the public sector.* Cape Town: Juta & Co. Ltd.

Wetly, G. 2008. The role of critical review in the revision of procedures. http://www.ivtnetwork.com/sites/default/files/RevisionProcedure_01.pdf (Accessed 31 July 2017).

GLOSSARY

accountability taking full responsibility, by a person or organisation, for actions or decisions taken or not taken by providing an explanation and accepting responsibility for the action or decision

administration the systematic process or activity of running a business or an organisation

administrative functions the process of organising people and resources in order to improve efficiency and effectiveness

attributes characteristics or character traits belonging to certain individuals

auxiliary functions extra assistance, especially referring to functions or jobs that the government might not undertake on its own

central government the highest level of government, the national government

communication the exchange of information by speaking, writing, or using some other medium

content refers to everything that forms part of governmental relations

control the process of ensuring that actual activities, actions or behaviour conform to set standards and procedures

control process a system where standards are set against which performance is measured, and corrective action is taken when deviations occur

decision-making the thought process of selecting a belief or option from those available

documentation records that are used to prove or make something official

equipment items that are used for a particular purpose

formal procedures steps that are well established or written and are used to achieve or accomplish a task

functional activities activities that are essential to support the physical, social and psychological well-being of a person

generic not specific, relating to a general class or group

government institutions facilities such as TVET colleges, universities or hospitals that are run by government, also known as public institutions

information services a service that provides knowledge about something

infrastructure physical facilities such as buildings, pipes, wires, roads and bridges

instrumental functions important skills and abilities that are necessary for one to perform a task

intergovernmental relationships the mutual relations that exist among government institutions or government structures

legal services the work done by lawyers and the courts

line functions the main purpose of an organisation, institution or department and the activities that define it

local government the lowest level of government; has authority on a municipal level

management functions the duties of people running an organisation

manager a person who is responsible for controlling or administering an organisation or a group of subordinates

methods processes that are used to achieve an objective

objectives things that need to be achieved

procedures systems of established steps that are taken to achieve an objective or to accomplish a task

protective wear clothing that is meant to prevent people from injury when performing a task

provincial government also known as provincial authority; government at the level of provinces

public accountability when government is answerable to the citizens for its actions, decisions and policies

public institutions the institutions that are owned or run by government; also known as government institutions

public liaison communication that takes place between officials working together in public institutions

public management a systematic way of managing people and resources within government or public institutions in order to achieve the goals of government

Public Protector (ombudsman) an official who is appointed by government to investigate complaints, by the public, against government agencies or officials

research investigations into the causes of things and how to solve problems

resistance to change the act of refusing or opposing transformation

state control systems that are put in place by government to ensure uniformity, efficiency and effectiveness in the delivery of services

stationery writing materials and office supplies

transport the means of moving people or goods from one place to another

work environment the conditions in which an employee operates

work procedures the process through which a task is carried out

ACKNOWLEDGEMENTS

Images

Page 2: Shutterstock 153987512 / Halfpoint; page 5: Shutterstock 200373776 / kungvery-lucky; page 6: Gareth Boden; page 7: Pixabay / Wokandapix; page 8: Shutterstock 157952597 / Bloomicon; page 9: Shutterstock 606447716 / designer491; page 11: Shutterstock 216280600 / SpeedKingz; page 12: Shutterstock 70168747 / tr3gin; Shutterstock 60407416 / David Woolfenden; page 13: Shutterstock 128236091 / Cartoon Resource; page 14: Shutterstock 232815346 / Rosie Apples; page 16: Shutterstock 213305518 / michaeljung; page 17: Shutterstock 513761224 / Constantin Stanciu; page 18: Shutterstock 18458581 / tkemot; page 18: Shutterstock 90761612 / BrunoWeltmann; page 19: Shutterstock 70154071 / takito; page 28: Shutterstock 479029780 / Monkey Business Images; page 30: Shutterstock / Andrey Popov; page 35: Shutterstock 123823738 / Dusit; page 35: Shutterstock 135361928 / michaeljung; page 36: Shutterstock 26119678 / apdesign; page 34: Gallo Images / Die Burger / Lulama Zenzile (0000085048); page 39: Shutterstock 209414842 / Albert H. Telch; page 40: Shutterstock 2080475 / ene; page 41: Shutterstock 16413013 / Fejas; page 42: APN557264 / Rodger Bosch; page 43: permission to reprint logo kindly granted by Public Protector South Africa; page 45: Shutterstock 107588237 / ESB Professional; page 48: Shutterstock 409908733 / Andrey Popov; page 51: permission to reprint logo kindly granted by the South African Reserve Bank; page 57: Shutterstock 92510755 / Michael Jung; page 60: Shutterstock 361871237 / Monkey Business Images; page 63: Shutterstock 480090436 / Rawpixel.com; page 64: Shutterstock 314862320 / Monkey Business Images; page 71: Shutterstock 151335653 / Michael Jung; page 72: Shutterstock 26052433 / gemphoto; page 72: Pixabay / Maylai; page 73: Shutterstock 362156894 / Rob Byron; page 73: Shutterstock 505117981 / ShutterStockStudio; page 75: Shutterstock 266367737 / Zerbor; page 76: Shutterstock 180005366 / jultud; page 76: Shutterstock 163017254 / Noci; page 77: Shutterstock 80591686 / Tyler Olson; page 79: Shutterstock 97844141 / StockLite; page 82: Shutterstock 164739686 / Ehrman Photographic; page 90: Shutterstock 478430395 / Monkey Business Images; page 91: Pixabay / Daniel B; page 92: Pixabay / jonathansautter; page 93: Shutterstock 15006421 / Monkey Business Images; page 94: Shutterstock 302622509 / Rawpixel.com; page 96: Shutterstock 42993643 / Scott Ward; page 97: Shutterstock / g-stock-studio; page 98: Shutterstock 262840061 / Jacob Lund; page 100: Shutterstock 129528119 / Leonard Zhukovsky, permission to reprint kindly granted by the South African Police Service; page 101: Shutterstock 126648614 / Monkey Business Images; page 102: Shutterstock 15840910 / Monkey Business Images; page 111: SASSA logo and image of Minister Susan Shabangu, permission to reprint kindly granted by SASSA; page 112: Shutterstock 109768634 / Richard Cavalleri; page 114: Shutterstock 198856475 / Intellistudies; page 115: Shutterstock 447912622 / Wavebreakmedia; page 116: Shutterstock 85960132 / kstudija; page 117: Shutterstock 134436836 / cleanfotos; page 118: permission to reprint kindly granted by the South African Police Service; page 119: Shutterstock 178148516 / Theodore Mattas; page 121: Pixabay / alohamalakhov; page 122: APN82183 sewage works – Guy Stubbs/ Independent Contributors/Africa Media Online; page 122: Shutterstock 276445445 / Riccardo Mayer; page 123: iStockphotos/rustynails; page 131: Shutterstock 108794750 / Michael Jung; page 133: Gallo Images / Foto24 / Denvor de Weep; page 134: Patricia Lague; page 136: Shutterstock 216343075 / Perfect Lazybones; page 138: Shutterstock / Andrea Izzotti; page 139: Shutterstock 189330617 / Duda Vasilii; page 141: Gallo Images / Hein von Horsten (GI_0022724); page 142: Gallo Images / Sowetan / Bafana Mahlangu (AV_00045526)

INDEX